The New-Paradigm Investor

Become a Successful Investor with a Winning-Edge Investment System

Ned Gandevani, PhD

iUniverse, Inc.
New York   Bloomington

The New Paradigm Investor
Become a Successful Investor with a Winning-Edge Investment System

iUniverse books may be ordered through booksellers or by contacting:

iUniverse
1663 Liberty Drive
Bloomington, IN 47403
www.iuniverse.com
1-800-Authors (1-800-288-4677)

Because of the dynamic nature of the Internet, any Web addresses or links contained in this book may have changed since publication and may no longer be valid. The views expressed in this work are solely those of the author and do not necessarily reflect the views of the publisher, and the publisher hereby disclaims any responsibility for them.

ISBN: 978-1-4401-2305-4 (pbk)
ISBN: 978-1-4401-2307-8 (cloth)
ISBN: 978-1-4401-2306-1 (ebk)

Library of Congress Control Number: 2009924360

Printed in the United States of America

iUniverse rev. date: 3/13/2009

To my mother, who taught me that dealing with adversity is the key to success.
And to the memory of my brother, who taught me the art of living.

Contents

Tables

Figures

Introduction

If you feel that you are living to work rather than working to live, there's really only one solution: you need to supplement your income with investments.

In today's rough and tumble economic environment, investing is no longer simply a choice—it's an absolute necessity. Why? Longer life spans, a greater imbalance between our incomes and expenses, and diminished purchasing power due to inflation to name only a few reasons.

Then why do so many people *not* invest? Aside from not understanding the importance of it, the most probable reason is that the majority of Americans either don't know how to invest or feel they lack the income to do so; in fact, most think they lack the financial resources to pay for their everyday expenses, let alone investments. If you identify with any or all of these scenarios, then you need to realize that a new day has dawned—a day in which investment is game for the average American and not just a luxury for the privileged few.

That's because the investment world, like so many other disciplines today, has undergone tremendous change. To be able to take full advantage of this changed system, however, you will need to gain a solid understanding of it, as well as the revised investment approach it requires. *The New Paradigm Investor* provides you with just such an understanding, along with winning strategies that you can use for successful investing in our modern day.

A new day

The new investment paradigm is all about achieving higher performance with less risk and in less time. In this paradigm, short-term, flexible investment management and decision-making is the order of the day, replacing protracted, impractical, inefficient long-term buy-and-hold strategies. For example, use of Exchange Traded Funds (ETFs) is swiftly replacing that of mutual funds, because twenty-first-century investors display more inclination toward risk in exchange for higher performance.

This paradigm shift in the investment world will be good news for investors who acknowledge and wisely utilize the new conceptual framework; they, quite simply, will enjoy better performance from their investments. Conversely, those who fail to recognize the shift, or recognize it but fail to adapt to it, will have a negative investment experience, because, plainly stated, the old investment methods will just not work anymore.

To be a successful investor, then—that is, to achieve great performance from your investments—you will need to change the way you were taught and trained to think about investing. And as a part of that, you will need to learn about the concepts, tools, and investment models that are more suitable to our current age of information and technology. Because the advent of technology (in particular, the Internet) has enabled us to obtain information faster than ever, there's no longer the need to get locked into a particular investment idea or stock as the old teaching insisted we do, buying and holding for the long term because it was the only way to be profitable. Doing otherwise, they said, would be trading only "noise"—that is, until several Wall Street darlings dropped from their historical highs to almost zeroes while we held them. So much for buy and hold.

In this book, you'll also learn the necessary steps to construct a winning portfolio according to the new-investment paradigm.

Part I: Investing for Survival

In Part I, we'll examine the crucial role of investing in today's world and learn why it is a practice that is no longer just for the privileged few but for everyone who desires economic prosperity, regardless of sex or socioeconomic background. In particular, we'll look at how investments relate to increased life expectancy and the resulting growth of the average retirement period; as part of that, we'll discover that wise investing is the best retirement plan for everyone, despite their income level. We'll also look at real-life examples, charts, and statistics to see how the ever-widening gap between income and inflation makes it increasingly difficult to manage our debt loads. Accordingly, we'll learn that smart investing is the only way to stay ahead of that debt, allowing us to enjoy the fruits of our hard work without worrying we might lose it during times of economic hardship (due to illness or job loss, for example).

Part I continues with an in-depth examination of the distinctive hallmarks of the old investment paradigm. Paramount among these features is the strategy known as buy and hold, which spells potential financial ruin for investors and is really not much of a strategy at all. Other features include strict reliance on brokers, a strong penchant for mutual funds (together with their hefty loads and fees), and infrequent monitoring of investment portfolios. We will then be introduced to the new paradigm, a revised way of thinking about investments that is characterized by speed and flexibility, encourages high-volume trading and online transactions, and, most important, promotes active short-term trading and the willingness to accept increased risk for better performance. This new paradigm offers a definitive benefit over the worn-out buy-and-hold strategy.

Finally, in Part I, we'll discuss the why's and how's of setting financial goals, and learn the key to achieving them: proper planning. We'll learn how to base financial goals on a number of personal factors, including age, and see examples of age-appropriate goals for the teen years all the way through retirement. We'll learn that financial goals need to be flexible and created with the proper motivation. And lastly, we'll learn how to manage our financial planning and goals by remembering a pneumonic device known as SMART and using the worksheet provided at the end of the chapter.

Part II: Constructing a Winning Investment Portfolio

In Part II, we'll shift our focus to examining how you as an individual investor can prosper in this new era, making your money work for you.

First, we will study the idea of risk. We'll discover that all investments come with certain inherent risks, the more common among them being credit, liquidity, inflation, currency, and political instability. We will learn how risk tolerance means different things to different people, depending on factors such as income, age, and personality; in turn, we'll see how those factors determine various risk-management strategies. Next, we'll learn techniques for analyzing our own risk tolerance and discover how that assessment can better position us to know what financial goals to set, both for ourselves and our families.

Part II continues by focusing on how to construct a winning portfolio. We will examine the different types of asset classes (cash, savings accounts, treasury bills, certificates of deposit, treasury bonds, corporate bonds, municipal bonds, and stocks) and how each relates to your particular portfolio. We will also discuss the standards for determining the viability of various stocks, exploring such ideas as profitability, liquidity, solvency, economic risk, and market risk, to help you decide which stocks belong in your portfolio—and which do not.

This will lead into the critical topic of finding the best strategies to diversify your portfolio. We will talk about a relatively new investment vehicle called Exchange Traded Funds (ETFs), along with its advantages and disadvantages, and the various methods for measuring ETFs to determine which ones might be right for you.

Part III: Monitoring Your Portfolio with a Winning-Edge System

A key practice of the new investment paradigm is more actively monitoring your investment portfolio. You should be able to review its securities or ETFs regularly and, at any given time, know which ones are at peak performance, which ones are not performing as expected, and which ones hold future potential. Then, accordingly, you should be able to rebalance your holdings for optimum performance, determining which ETFs to keep and which ones to sell.

For this reason, Part III covers the two primary methods of monitoring stocks in your portfolio: fundamental analysis and technical analysis. Fundamental analysis seeks an undervalued security to buy and an expensive or overvalued security to sell. Similarly, technical analysis looks at oversold conditions for a security to buy and an overbought condition to sell.

Starting with a brief overview of fundamental analysis, we'll find that this is primarily used in situations where we want to move from a general perspective of a portfolio down to a more specific one. We'll then explore the many facets of technical analysis, learning how to understand and interpret related bar charts, technical indicators, momentum indicators, oscillators, and trend lines.

The remainder of the chapter studies a wide range of analytical tools, including moving averages and oscillators, focusing in particular on the importance of oscillators—how they work and how to use them to your advantage.

Finally, we'll discuss how to use the Winning-Edge Investment System to generate better investment performance, applying the knowledge and tools discussed in the book thus far (from assessing risk tolerance to diversifying your portfolio to analyzing the market) and illustrating through real-life scenarios and examples how to invest with success in these new times.

Part IV: Understanding Investment Psychology

Knowing what to do is only one pillar of successful investing. The other pillar is how you apply that knowledge. Learning investment psychology is vital to recognizing those mental pitfalls that could hurdle your performance despite your in-depth knowledge of investing. That's why, in Part IV, we go over this psychology, including decision traps you should be aware of as you attempt to achieve your financial goals and become a successful new-paradigm investor.

Part I

Investing for Survival

Chapter 1:
Investment for Survival

Science continues to explore brave new frontiers in medicine, enabling us not only to live longer than ever before but also to enjoy our longer lives more with better health. Meanwhile, we are experiencing an ever-increasing disparity between our incomes and our expenses. The combination of these two realities in our lives today should certainly require us to appreciate the need for wise investing.

However, most of us still do not recognize this need. Most of us would prefer to use our money to satisfy seemingly urgent cravings for instantaneous, temporary pleasure than to invest for rainy days. And as ridiculous as that may sound, it's not surprising when you think about the fact that we are surrounded by Madison Avenue's powerful advertising, by commercial enterprises that promise to fulfill our dreams if we just acquire enough of their latest products and gadgets. It is thus that "living for the moment" has become a trendy and prevalent motto in the majority of our cultural sectors.

On the other hand, some of us realize that we'll have to pay dearly later on for such rash thinking and behavior. If you are one such person, keep reading. In this chapter, I aim to demystify the common misconception that you should consider investing only when you are wealthy and thriving.

You live longer

Life expectancy has increased drastically in the twentieth century. This is mainly due to the converged influence of factors such as higher public awareness about health issues, nutrition, and medical advancement in recent years.

In the United States in 1999, the average life expectancy was estimated to be 77 years of age: 79.4 years for women and 73.6 years for men, with lower life expectancy for African Americans—67.2 years for men and 74.7 years for women (1). By some estimates, if that increase continued at its current pace, the average American could expect to live past 100 by the end of this century. And in fact, revolutionary advances and discoveries in health and medicine are projected to increase the average life span up to 120 years. On top of all that, the required minimum retirement age has increased from 62 to 65 and, in practice, now stands at about 72 years of age.

While these record-setting highs are indeed good news, they also indicate a greater need for Americans to save and invest in order to enjoy longer lives and longer retirements; after all, it certainly wouldn't be fun to live longer without the proper accommodations and financial resources.

Your expenses grow faster than your income

I don't like to draw a gloomy picture. I believe in being optimistic about your financial future. But you need to be realistic as well. That's why it's imperative to understand that investment is no longer a choice; it's not just one option among many. These days, investment is a necessity for economic survival.

But maybe you were brought up thinking that investing is something only for the well-off, that you shouldn't worry about investing because you're having a hard enough time just making ends meet. Well, that's precisely the point! As salespeople love to say, it's something that you can't afford *not* to do. And if you honestly evaluate your financial situation, you will likely see why. Go ahead, take a quick look. You'll probably notice an alarming trend: your expenses are increasing much faster than your income. This thought alone is scary, let alone the though that if you don't supplement your income soon, things are destined to go from bad to worse.

According to the Bureau of Labor Statistics' 2006 Consumer Expenditure Survey, the average income increased from just over $58,700 in 2005 to just over $60,500 in 2006; meanwhile, total expenses increased from about $46,400 to nearly $48,400. As exhibited in Table 1.1, the amount of total expenses does not include the 25 percent taxes the income is subjected to. Conversely, the increase in Personal Disposable Income (PDI), an amount figured by subtracting personal taxes, was only 3.10 percent in 2006, while the increase in expenses was 4.29 percent (2).

	2005	2006
Income		
Wages	$58,712	$60,533
Total Income	$58,712	$60,533
Expenses		
Housing	$5,204	$5,270
Utilities	5,931	6,111
Food	8,344	8,508
Transportation	2,664	2,766
Medical	1,886	1,874
Clothing	2,388	2,376
Entertainment	4,823	5,129
Other	4,823	5,129
Total Expenses	$46,409	$48,398
Cash surplus (or deficit)	$12,303	$12,135

Table 1.1. 2006 Consumer Expenditure Survey Results

Here's a real-life example to illustrate my point. Your expenses are increasing at an average rate of 10 percent per year. If you think this is unrealistic, I urge you to consider the average inflation rate of about 3 percent. That doesn't include rental expenses—or if you are a homeowner, local real estate taxes—which increase by about 5 to 10 percent. Health insurance, car insurance, and fuel increases can easily add up to another 4 percent. So a 10 percent yearly increase is not far-fetched. Now, here's where it gets a bit frightening: you're lucky if your income increases by an average of 3 percent per year.

Let's demonstrate these percentages with some fictitious amounts. Assume that you're just starting out and your yearly income and yearly expenses each total $100. How long do you suppose it would it take before you'd need to double your income just to cover your expenses? Probably not as long as you think. See Table 1.2 and Figure 1.1 below to see the results of this annual 10 percent increase in expenses versus a 3 percent increase in income.

Year	Expenses ($)	Income ($)
1	100	100
2	110	103
3	121	106
4	133	109
5	146	112
6	161	116
7	177	119
8	195	123
9	215	127

Table 1.2. Annual growth of $100 of expenses by 10 percent versus 3 percent

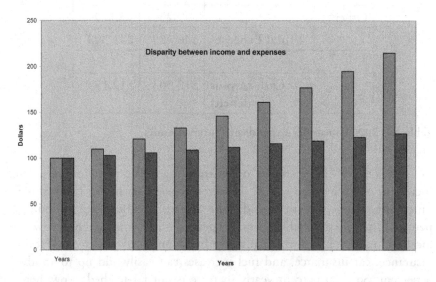

Figure 1.1. The hypothetical disparity in annual growth between $100 in income and $100 in expenses over 9 years

As Table 1.2 demonstrates, it would take only 9 years for your expenses to double, ballooning to $219, while your income increased to a paltry $127. Do you see how difficult it could become just to meet your basic daily needs? How mere trips to the grocery store could become frightening, with the price of food—even the gas to get to there—constantly rapidly increasing? How can anyone afford to live under these circumstances?

And these numbers speak only to the ability to meet daily needs, to those needs that will always be there, to needs that can at least be predicted and budgeted for. But what about unforeseen expenses? For example, your car breaks down and the service station informs you it's the transmission. If you're already on a tight budget, where do you get the extra several thousand dollars it will take to fix the problem? Even if you have, or had, a "rainy day" fund, it's amazing how quickly it can be depleted, especially if you have a lot of rainy days. And keep in mind that a broken car is only one of countless pitfalls that could easily knock you off your financial moorings.

So, short of immoral or illegal activities such as selling drugs or robbing banks, there's only one realistic solution to increasing your income: investing. Investing helps, first, just to cope with everyday expenses and, second, to store away extra for those inevitable rainy days; the bottom line being that investing is barely a choice; as mentioned earlier, these days it's a necessity.

Inflation is diminishing your purchasing power

As just demonstrated, the cost of living is rising much faster than the average income. This cost-of-living increase is caused by inflation, or the ever-increasing value of the dollar. Because of this direct correlation between inflation and cost of living, the most widely used tool to gauge inflation is actually the Consumer Price Index (CPI), a measure of the average change in prices of goods and services consumed in a year (3). In fact, the CPI is considered so reliable that it is often even used as a barometer of the effectiveness of governmental monetary and fiscal policy; for example, to adjust the effect of inflation on wages, salaries, pensions, or regulated or contracted prices. In short, then, due to inflation, the prices of goods and services increase, and it is the rise of those prices that's measured by the CPI.

Figures 1.2 and 1.3 below provide a comparison of CPI and inflation. Figure 1.2 shows historical annual CPI changes, while Figure 1.3 gives historical annual inflation rates. Comparing these figures confirms that there is a direct relationship between the two phenomena: when the CPI percentage increases, the inflation rate also increases; likewise, the two simultaneously decrease. For example, from 1913 to 1920, the CPI followed a steady uphill slope only to hit a sharp decrease in 1921; the inflation rate for that time period followed an identical pattern. This correlation explains why the CPI is used to measure inflation of daily living expenses as experienced by consumers (3).

Figure 1.2. U.S. Consumer Price Index (4)

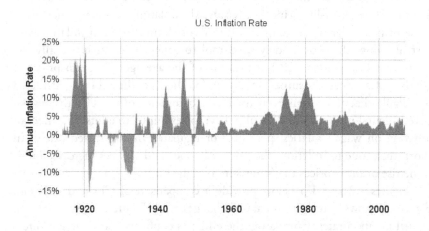

Figure 1.3. U.S. Historical Inflation (5)

In addition to comparison data, each chart in itself holds useful information about the cost of living and inflation over the years. For example, you may have noticed in Figure 1.2 that, over the long term, the average CPI has substantially increased. The first record of CPI in 1913, for instance, held an average of 9.9, whereas by 2007 the average was over 207;

and, in particular, we saw a substantial increase from the 1970s onward. Figure 1.2 also shows that the percentage change was more volatile in the early 1900s than in the later half of the century up to the present: from 1916 to 1932, the average CPI ranged from about 18 percent to about -10 percent; conversely, from 1983 to 2007, the annual average ranged only between 1.6 to 5.4 percent.

Now look at Table 1.3 below. This table has been constructed based on data from the U.S. Department of Labor, Bureau of Labor Statistics, and portrays a definite increase in cumulative CPI since 1970, just less than forty years ago. You can use Table 1.3 to calculate how much a dollar from a previous year is worth today. For instance, in 2007, a dollar from 1999 would have cost $1.23; a dollar from 1900 would have cost $24.61. Accordingly, the same goods or services that would cost you $435.49 today would have been just $5.84 in 1970. If this upward trend in prices continues, your income will need to increase more than fourfold—about 435 percent, to be exact—over the next forty years. That's about 10 percent per year just to meet your current expenses. In summary, you don't need to look hard to see that inflation has substantially increased over the decades.

From January, in the year ...	To January, in the year ...	Average CPI for the beginning year	Cumulative CPI from the beginning year to January 2007
2007	2007	2.85	2.85
2006	2007	3.24	2.08
2005	2007	3.39	6.14
2004	2007	2.68	9.30
2003	2007	2.27	11.40
2002	2007	1.59	14.29
2001	2007	2.83	15.60
2000	2007	3.38	19.91
1999	2007	2.16	23.20
1998	2007	1.55	25.26
1997	2007	2.34	27.23
1996	2007	2.93	31.03
1995	2007	2.81	34.67
1994	2007	2.61	38.45
1993	2007	2.96	41.95
1992	2007	3.03	46.57
1991	2007	4.25	50.38
1990	2007	5.39	58.88
1989	2007	4.83	67.15
1988	2007	4.08	74.95
1987	2007	3.66	82.03
1986	2007	1.91	84.69
1985	2007	3.55	91.86
1984	2007	4.30	98.64
1983	2007	3.22	106.97
1982	2007	6.16	114.65
1981	2007	10.35	132.66
1980	2007	13.58	160.17

	1979	2007	11.22	196.36
	1978	2007	7.62	223.87
	1977	2007	6.50	246.01
	1976	2007	5.75	264.06
	1975	2007	9.20	288.51
	1974	2007	11.03	334.37
	1973	2007	6.16	375.15
	1972	2007	3.27	392.50
	1971	2007	4.30	408.58
	1970	2007	5.84	435.49

Table 1.3. Yearly increases in CPI (6)

The goods and services represented in the CPI have been classified by the Bureau of Labor Statistics into more than 200 categories, which are then divided among the following eight major groups (3):

- Food and Beverages
- Housing
- Apparel
- Transportation
- Medical Care
- Recreation
- Education and Communication
- Other Goods and Services

Because the published CPI is based on such *sets* of particular goods and services, keep in mind that it may not truly reflect your real-life expenditure increase in every category. For example, if you have a longer commute to work than the average American, you could see your costs soar higher than your typical fellow citizen's. If you take a lot of vacations, increases in the price of travel will have more of an impact on you than on your neighbor who barely ever leaves the house. By the same token, maybe your neighbor buys a new car every two years, while you've been content with the same vehicle for the past five. In this case, increases in automobile prices will strain his budget while it won't affect you at all. So to a large degree, your personal CPI will be a direct function of your lifestyle.

Table 1.4 depicts the annual percentage changes in several of these different categories of expenditures, to give you a better picture of how your lifestyle—now and in the future—affects your own personal CPI. It clearly shows, for example, that energy, transportation, and food are some of the highest-costing items. So in that vein, it also shows what would happen to you financially should you, let's say, decide to have more children. Perhaps you'd need to buy a bigger vehicle, which would mean bigger expenses at the gas pump. Children also eat a lot and, in fact, eat more the bigger they grow, so it's only natural that you'd increase spending in the "food and beverages" category.

Expenditure Category	Percentage change 12 months ended in December							
	2000	2001	2002	2003	2004	2005	2006	2007
All items	3.4	1.6	2.4	1.9	3.3	3.4	2.5	4.1
Food and beverages	2.8	2.8	1.5	3.5	2.6	2.3	2.2	4.8
Housing	4.3	2.9	2.4	2.2	3.0	4.0	3.3	3.0
Apparel	-1.8	-3.2	-1.8	-2.1	-.2	-1.1	.9	-.3
Transportation	4.1	-3.8	3.8	.3	6.5	4.8	1.6	8.3
Medical care	4.2	4.7	5.0	3.7	4.2	4.3	3.6	5.2
Recreation	1.7	1.5	1.1	1.1	.7	1.1	1.0	.8
Education and communication	1.3	3.2	2.2	1.6	1.5	2.4	2.3	3.0
Other goods and services	4.2	4.5	3.3	1.5	2.5	3.1	3.0	3.3
Special indexes:								
Energy	14.2	-13.0	10.7	6.9	16.6	17.1	2.9	17.4
Energy commodities	15.7	-24.5	23.7	6.9	26.7	16.7	6.1	29.4
Energy services	12.7	-1.5	.4	6.9	6.8	17.6	-.6	3.4
All items less energy	2.6	2.8	1.8	1.5	2.2	2.2	2.5	2.8
Food	2.8	2.8	1.5	3.6	2.7	2.3	2.1	4.9
All items less food and energy	2.6	2.7	1.9	1.1	2.2	2.2	2.6	2.4

Table 1.4. Itemized percentage increases in expenditures in the twelve months ending in December, from 2000 to 2007 (7)

Housing: a major source of financing

For several years, until 2006, the price of real estate grew by substantial increases; some might even say by leaps and bounds. Millions of homeowners took advantage of this real estate "bubble" and tapped into their home equity to finance daily expenditures, essentially using their homes as ATM machines to sustain increasing expenses with stagnant income. The result: between 2002 and 2007, American households borrowed $4.4 trillion in home loans, bolstering home mortgage debt to a staggering $10.4 trillion.

In addition, household debt, which is primarily composed of mortgage debt and credit (credit cards, auto loans, etc.) rose to about $12.82 trillion in 2006, a whopping 9 percent increase over the prior year. (See Figure 1.4.) The following year, household debt increased another 9 percent to $12.8 trillion, $9.7 trillion of which was mortgage debt (8).

No wonder when the home-based ATMs were closed due to the subprime meltdown and credit crunch, millions of Americans lost their homes and now face a grim financial future.

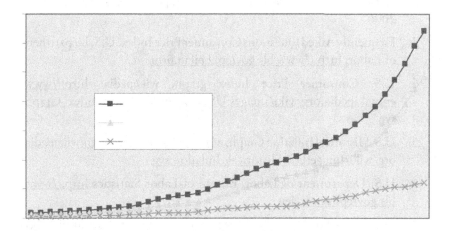

Figure 1.4. The U.S. Household Debt Ratio (8)

All in all, millions of Americans are suffering from a lack of income growth and are struggling to keep up with daily expenses. So to supplement their incomes, a vast majority of Americans—about 70 percent, according to some estimates—are borrowing. And they are borrowing not only against the equity in their homes, but also through credit cards and financing options. And thanks to the ridiculously high interest rates of some of these credit cards and financing plans, such borrowers are actually making their situations worse, digging themselves into a financial hole. And then instead of climbing out of it, they just keep digging more and more deeply, buying today with the hope of paying tomorrow.

Borrowing is a recipe for disaster. It requires that you live beyond your means and puts you into a vicious cycle of debt that only goes from bad to worse. And it prevents you from tackling the root of the problem: lack of sufficient income.

For this reason, the next chapter will look at some of the vital signs of Americans' financial health.

Chapter 1 References

1. Hoyert, Kochanek, and Murphy, 1999

2. Bureau of Labor Statistics, Consumer Expenditure Survey (Annual) 2006

3. Frequently Asked Questions Consumer Price Index, U.S. Department of Labor; http://www.bls.gov/cpi.cpifaq.htm

4. U.S. Consumer Price Index graph, wikepedia; http://www.en.wikipedia.org.wiki/Images:US_Consumer_Price_Index_Graph.svg

5. U.S. Historical Inflation Graph, wikepedia; http://www.en.wikipedia.org/wiki/Image:US_Historical_Inflation.svg

6. U.S. Department of Labor, Bureau of Labor Statistics http://www.bls.gov/cpi/#overview

7. Department of Labor U.S. Department of Labor, Bureau of Labor Statistics http://www.bls.gov/news.release/cpi.nr0.htm

8. U.S. Household Debt Ratio; http://www.federalreserve.gov/releases/z1/20061207/z1.pdf

Chapter 2:
Consumer Debt Overview

In order to understand the situation that the average household is in, we must first examine the situation that our economy is in. According to statistics from the U.S. Treasury, the national debt as of January 2008 was about $9.24 trillion dollars and still growing exponentially as a result of interest the federal government owes to the Federal Reserve (1). Of this amount, about 55 percent, or $5.13 trillion, is held by the public, which as of July 2001, had an annual estimated population of 301 million (2). Doing the math with these two figures, we can see that the average individual debt is about $17,000.

Here's another way of looking at consumer debt: According to the Federal Reserve's 2006 Consumer Credit Report (3), total credit of American consumers was $2,387.5 billion. And according to the 2006 U.S. Census, the number of households was 116,001,000 (4). Those numbers mean the average household debt was approximately $21,600, excluding mortgages. In addition, the median household income that year, according to the census report, was $48,201 household (5). Using these last two figures, you can calculate the average annual debt safety ratio of Americans. This ratio measures total debt payments on outstanding mortgage and consumer debt as it relates to disposable household income, and should not exceed 20 percent. Yet approximately 45 percent of household income is spent on debt incurred by the household, which is well above the 20 percent that an average household should handle. Of course, these numbers are not an accurate depiction for any one particular household or individual; nevertheless, it is conclusive evidence that the United States is heavily in debt.

Figure 2.1 shows consumer credit outstanding from 2003 to 2007. (Learn more about the definition of "consumer credit outstanding" further down in this section.) For the past 4 years, there has been a steady increase of the consumer credit outstanding of around 5 percent. In 2007, the credit outstanding was at $2,519.5 billion, a 5.5 percent increase from the previous year. From 2005 to 2006, it increased 4.5 percent; from 2004 to 2005, 4.3 percent; and from 2003 to 2004, 5.5 percent (6).

Of that credit outstanding, nonrevolving credit was used most—around 63 percent of the time—as opposed to revolving credit. Whether it's a credit card, a consumer loan, a student loan, a mortgage, or home equity, more and more people are using credit and falling increasingly into debt. To help offset this debt, consumers need to invest in order to survive.

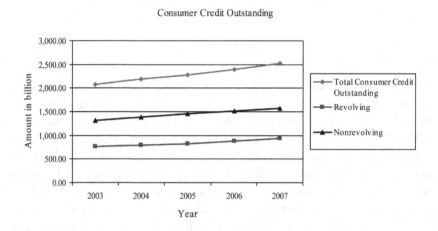

Figure 2.1. Outstanding consumer credit according to the Federal Reserve Board (5).

You may be wondering whether the American economic situation could really be all that bad. The *New York Times* recently asked the same question, running a story that explored the consequences of Americans' credit habits. Some of the results were, to say the least, startling. In 1990, the average American household with an outstanding credit card balance owed $2,550; by the end of 2003, that figure ballooned to $7,520, an increase of nearly 200 percent. In addition, the total amount being charged to these credit cards saw an even bigger increase—up 350 percent from 1990. And these figures include only credit card balances and charges, while the typical American household also has mortgage debt, student loans, and automobile loans.

The problem would not be so serious if average salaries were keeping up. But just to stay even with the average debt load during that 13-year period from 1990 to 2003, the average income would have to grow from $35,000 to $122,500, which is a 350 percent increase. Unfortunately, the Bureau of Labor Statistics reports that incomes are up by only 188 percent.

All of this is bad news for consumers, but it's a gold mine for credit card companies. The *Times* reports that pretax profits for credit card companies have grown 360 percent from 1990 to 2003, while fee revenues have grown 250 percent. At that rate, they're not liable to change their approach anytime soon.

Now, couple that avalanche of easily available (though very expensive) credit with the sharply rising mortgage default rate, and you have a situation where more and more people are living off of their credit cards. Statistics reveal some startling figures:

- Total credit card debt in the US: $943 billion
- Number of credit cards: 1.2 billion
- Number of credit cards per person: 7
- Average debt per household: $9,840
- Annual debt service cost per household: $1,500
- Percent of households with no credit cards: 7
- Percent of households that pay their credit card bill monthly: 32
- Percent of card holders that owe more than $25,000: 8
- Average household savings rate: 0.5 percent

Let's try to put all of this into perspective. To properly gauge consumer debt obligations, there are several important figures and ratios. You may think that these indicators are important only for economists, or other academics who study such things. But that would be a big mistake! It is vital for you, the average citizen, to understand these statistics as well. As you will see, they have a direct impact on your personal finances and your ability to support yourself and your family. Let's briefly examine each of these key economic indicators.

- **Consumer credit outstanding.** This figure, which we just touched on briefly above, represents the amount of money that consumers owe to their creditors at any given time. At the end of 2005, this figure reached an astronomical level of more than $2.1 trillion, *not* including mortgage debt! Other consumer credit outstanding data indicates that Americans are doing little to lower their debt load, even when recession strikes.

- **Personal bankruptcy filings.** Personal bankruptcy filings have steadily run alongside unabated increases in consumer debt. Consider this sobering statistic: more than 1.6 million Americans filed for bankruptcy during the 12 months ending in June 30, 2005. That's more than quadruple the number from 20 years earl*ier* in 1985. The message of this dramatic increase is clear: Americans are spending more than they earn. That doesn't necessarily mean that people are living extravagantly. What it does necessarily mean is that the cost of living these days is quickly outpacing people's ability to earn a living. Moreover, bankruptcy is no longer a trend that so disproportionately represents primarily the young. The *Wall Street Journal* reported that middle-aged Americans now increasingly find themselves filing for bankruptcy. That only goes to prove that being established in the work force for many years is no longer a reliable bulwark against financial hardship. In today's economy, disaster can strike anyone, young or old, often with little or no warning. It isn't something that happens only to "other" people.

- **Ratio of household liabilities to net worth.** This ratio is a realistic measure of people's ability to pay off their debts. It measures the capacity that people have, by tapping into their accumulated wealth, to liquidate debt. As with the other indicators, this one has shown substantially increasing numbers this decade, hitting a record high in the last quarter of 2005. Much of this unprecedented growth has been fueled by surging mortgage debt, which has jumped a whopping 97 percent since 1999. That means that the safety net that many families have been relying on is slowly eroding, and it may not be there for them much longer—or worse, when they need it most.

- **Debt service ratio and financial obligations ratio.** These two ratios are closely related. The first one measures the share of disposable income committed to the payment of mortgage and consumer debt. The second ratio, which is a more comprehensive statistic that was introduced by the Federal Reserve in 2003, further includes other common household obligations such as rent, auto leases, property taxes, and homeowners' insurance. Though both ratios declined in the fourth quarter of 2005, they are nonetheless still close to record highs. In other words, consumer debt obligations are more daunting than ever before. It's little wonder that so many people literally find themselves living on the brink of financial ruin (7).

To avoid this very unpleasant (yet very real!) possibility of overwhelming debt, you thin, you will need to earn extra income. Maybe you could work more hours. But honestly, how many more hours could you afford to work without hurting your health, your personal life, or your family? Remember, there are only so many hours in a day and so many days in a week. And yet many Americans try to pursue this as a realistic option. No wonder researchers tell us that the majority of Americans have fewer close friends than they used to; there's no time left for a social life. Friends are left in the lurch, as we find ourselves spending more and more time on the job. So we're back to the same old dilemma.

What's left? Short of robbing a bank, your best and most viable choice is to invest. Investing will help you generate money to supplement your regular income.

Women need to invest, too

Once upon a time it was just assumed that at a certain age, a woman would get married and stay home to raise her children. Her husband would earn the family's income and take care of all of the household's financial obligations. As we know, those days are long since past. Women now hold important positions in the nation's work force, and their incomes are just as important as their husbands' for sustaining the family's standard of living. Moreover, consider the following:

1. Women live longer than men.
2. There is a 50 percent divorce rate.
3. About 80 percent of women at some point in their lives are solely responsible for their financial affairs (8).

For these reasons and more, women need to learn about investing.

Chapter 2 References

1. Monthly Statement of the Public Debt of the United States, U.S. Treasury: http://www.treasurydirect.gov/govt/reports/pd/mspd/2008/opds012008.pdf

2. Annual Estimates of the Population for the United States, Regions, States and Puerto Rico, U.S. Census Bureau: http://www.census.gov/popest/states/tables/NST-EST2007-01.xls

3. Consumer Credit Federal Reserve Statistical Release; 2008, Feb. 7, http://www.federalreserve.gov/releases/g19/Current/

4. United States S1101 Households and Families, U.S. Census Bureau; http://factfinder.census.gov/servlet/STTable?_bm=y&-geo_id =01000US&-qr_name=ACS_2006_EST_G00_S1101&-ds_name=ACS_2006_EST_G00_&-_lang=en&-redoLog=false

5. Income, Poverty, and Health Insurance Coverage in the United States: 2006, U.S. Census Bureau; http://www.census.gov/prod/2007pubs/p60-233.pdf

6. Outstanding consumer credit according to the Federal Reserve Board; http://www.federalreserve.gov/releases/g19/Current/

7. Consumer Credit Federal Reserve Statistical Release; 2008, Feb. 7, http://www.federalreserve.gov/releases/g19/Current/

8. Perspectives on Recent Trends in Consumer Debt, Andrew Kish, Federal Reserve Bank of Philadelphia, June 2006;

9. http://www.philadelphiafed.org/pcc/papers/2006/D2006June ConsumerDebtCover.pdf

10. Women and Investing, Lauren Ohayon (2006); http://www.pbs.org/wnet/moneyshow/cover/102000.html

Chapter 3:
The Twenty-First-Century
Investment Paradigm

In general, a paradigm is a set of assumptions and values—a conceptual model that encompasses ways of doing things and seeing realties. As such, a person's practices are determined by the prevailing paradigm.

More specifically then, an *investment paradigm* constitutes all of the practices, advice, and popular thinking regarding investing. In that vein, the old investment paradigm constitutes the following ideas: invest for a long time using the buy-and-hold strategy and use mutual funds as a typical investment vehicle In contrast, the new twenty-first-century paradigm emphasizes the flaws of buy-and-hold strategies and recognizes that mutual funds are not proper vehicles for most investors; instead, its set of ideas revolves around speed, optimization, and maximum performance with less cost and commissions and more flexibility and maneuverability.

Perhaps one of the greatest contrasts between the old and new paradigms is the new value of speed, which drastically contradicts once-esteemed buy-and-hold strategy. Why? Consider this: You invest your hard-earned money in a mutual fund. Always taught that you should invest for the long term, you wait and wait. By the time you are ready to retire, you find that all of your gains have been wiped out due to market corrections, which means you're left with nothing as you enter into your "golden years"—except hollow dreams and empty pockets. If only you'd sold your stock when it was at an all-time high and then repurchased it at a much lower price, you wouldn't be in this dilemma.

Essentially, the value of speed in the new investment paradigm says, "Don't let this happen to you. Or, at the very least, don't let it happen to you again."

Old investment paradigm

To help us better appreciate the significance of the new investment paradigm, we must first review the main traits of the old one. Here are

1. Buy and hold. As mentioned, one of the signature elements of the old investment paradigm is an almost obsessive fixation on the buy-and-hold strategy. Every investment book and college course has always taught that you should buy a good stock and hold it until you retire or need to sell it. What they didn't tell you, however, was that by the time you sell your stock or investment portfolio, its value may be even lower than what you bought it for.

The problem with the buy-and-hold strategy preached by universities and investment academies is that it pays no attention to an investor's particulars, such as personal needs and timing. I don't know about you, but I'm not sure if I would want to hold my investment in unexpected events such as death, illness, or job loss. Or, conversely, what if I'd retired sometime in 2002 and had to pull out my investment and liquidate my equity positions only then? I'd have lost about 40 to 70 percent of my portfolio value if all of it had been invested in the equity. So in reality, the buy-and-hold strategy may have never truly held any benefit for most of us. And these days, it may well be just a recipe for disaster.

Let's take a look at a real-life example. Throughout the year 2000, there were over 22,000 stock recommendations by professional analysts. Fewer than sixty of those were recommendations to sell. That same year, however, Wall Street suffered one of its worst markets in 35 years. The "experts," while selling any of their own stocks that were tanking, as common sense would dictate, continued to advise their customers not to sell. Their motive for giving such advice was the traditional idea that unless you are extremely savvy in the ups and downs of the market, your best bet as the "average" investor is just to hang on to your portfolio; eventually, the market will adjust and everything will be fine.

Proponents of this buy-and-hold approach will try to support their claims by pointing out statistical averages of stocks over the past 50 to 100 years. There are several flaws to their theory, however. First, the Dow Jones Index, for example, was not the same set of companies today as it was 100 years ago; in fact, the index is re-adjusted every few years, which means you didn't really buy and hold. That is, you're not really holding the stock you bought. Rather, the portfolio you purchased is being frequently adjusted along the way.

Second, who has 50 to 100 years to grow a portfolio? Perhaps you have 20 or 30 years at best, that is, if you want to enjoy your profit before you're too old. Realizing this realistic time horizon in itself introduces another risk you may not have thought about. Here's an example: had you started your buy-and-hold portfolio of technology stocks in March of 2000, or in 1929, or in the early 1970s, or in 1987, or at many other similar times in between, you would have experienced such a crippling loss that you may not have recovered within your lifetime.

In fact, many "blue chip" stocks that were traditionally Wall Street's darlings for long-term investments—for example, Zenith and PanAm or, in recent years, WorldCom and Enron (which never recovered after its fall)—would have indeed been disastrous for your investment portfolio. And these are not isolated cases. In fact, you'd likely be surprised by how many companies that for all the world appear to be reputable and profitable are harboring secrets that might one day destroy them. For example, the PBS show *Frontline* explored the implosion of one of America's best-known corporations, Sunbeam. According to PBS, Sunbeam CEO Al Dunlap, in the late 1990s, used simple accounting tricks to paint a picture of a turnaround in earnings that didn't exist. With a pay package that included more than 7 million shares and options, Dunlap stood to make more than $200 million personally if he could keep Sunbeam's stock price flying. But in the spring of 1998, when Dunlap and his team ran out of tricks, Sunbeam corrected its books, declared bankruptcy, and the stock price plunged from $53 at its peak to just pennies. If you'd been an unfortunate stockholder in Sunbeam at the time, or in any one of the many similar companies that are out there, adhering to the rigid buy-and-hold strategy as you'd been taught to do, you'd have paid a heavy price. Even if the law (or in most cases, just the natural dynamics of the marketplace) had been able catch up with them, it would have been too late for you by the time they had. Table 3.1 depicts how much of a gain you would require just to make up for such investment capital losses.

Loss of capital (%)	Gain needed to recover (%)
5	5.3
10	11.1
15	17.6
20	25.0
25	33.3
30	42.9
35	53.8
40	66.7
45	81.8
50	100.0
55	122.0
60	150.0

Table 3.1. The return required to compensate for any possible loss of investment capital

The lack of flexibility that is so integral to the buy-and-hold strategy, combined with the reality of such a bear market—one that can permanently cripple a buy-and-hold portfolio—is one reason why this strategy is fading into oblivion; it's become more evident than ever that buy and hold was never a proven or even reliable strategy in the first place. A bear market which is the opposite of a bull market occurs when the stock market drops for a prolonged period of time, usually by twenty percent or more. This decline and sell off is due to few factors such as market psychology, high and sometimes unrealistic valuations of stocks and low earnings by companies. After paying dearly for stocks, investors realize that companies can not sustain estimated earnings and decide to sell their holdings. As market falls, more market participants note their losses and decide to sell their stocks. This creates a vicious cycle of selling. A good example for a prolonged bear market is the 1970's which market moved sideways for over a decade.

2. Invest for the long term. This advice is in directly line with the buy-and-hold strategy. You have likely always heard that stocks perform better over the long term and result in loss if held for a short term. In the old investment paradigm, short-term trading is considered "noise" trading.

"Long term" is a subjective concept. How long is long term? The old paradigm proponents try to convince you of the merits of long-term investing by presenting statistics about stock-market performance over about a hundred years. They calculate average yearly performance and argue that despite all of the major market corrections in history—including some as recent as 1930, 1976, 1987, 2000, and 2007-08 —yearly performance has been consistently positive for the "long term." And then they conclude by saying that to enjoy market return, you should invest for the long term and avoid market timing.

However, glancing over any long-term or short-term market price charts, you could easily conclude that markets don't go straight up or down. As an example, let us consider the Standard & Poor's (S&P) 500 chart in Figure 3.1. The S&P 500 index is similar to the Dow Jones averages to the extend that they both are designed to obtain the overall performance of the market. This index is based on 500 LargeCap companies This chart indicates that if you had to withdraw some or all of your investment at any point in 2002, you'd have lost close to 40 percent of your investment just since August 2000. And according to American Association of Retired People, AARP (1), a dollar invested in an index fund in March 2000 would have been worth 55 cents in August 2002. Further, $700 billion in retirement savings was depleted in the 2000–2002 market correction. Total loss in the last three years of 2000-2002 amounted to $7 trillion.

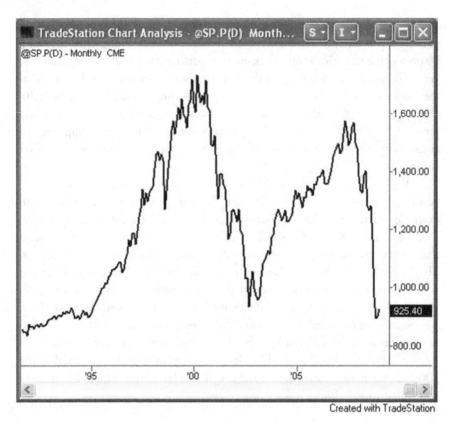

Figure 3.1. Standard & Poor's 500 Stock Index performance over the past 20 years

As of the time this book was written in November 2008, the market has been unable to recoup its losses since 2000. Furthermore, if you had invested in the market for the long term, by 2008, you'd have lost a good portion of your hard-earned savings.

The year 2008 may be recorded as the worst year ever for the phenomenon of wealth destruction for investors and traders. Despite the massive US Government $820 billion bail out, the stock market has continued its spiral selloff and meltdown. Just about one year ago the S&P 500, an index of 500 large cap common stocks published since 1957, made an intraday all time high at 1,576.09 on October 11, 2007. As of November 21, the date of this writing, the S&P 500 index since peaking at an all-time closing high of 1,565.15 on Oct. 9, 2007, has lost 52%. The Dow has lost nearly 47% since closing at an all-time high of 14,164.53 on the same day. Since hitting a bull market high of 2,859.12 on Oct. 31, 2007, the NASDAQ has lost 54%.

Investors suffered a great blow as the S&P 500 plunged to an 11-1/2 year low as fears of a prolonged recession sparked a massive selloff and closed at its lowest point sine April 14, 1997. However, as investors experience their biggest losses ever in their pension funds and investment portfolios, some financial gurus and advisors continue to spew out "stay the course" advice. They dispense this so-called wisdom as if we didn't hear their irresponsible and downright fraudulent advice on some of Wall Street's long term holdings like Lucent, WorldCom, Enron, Merrill Lynch, and Bear Stearns.

According to the reports, in October 2008 alone a great deal of consumer wealth was dissipated as a result of recent stock market losses - consumers do not have as much money to spend. Unemployment has been rising as well so there is less money in the economy. Without this money circulating in the economy, and without anything to replace it, it is hard to see where the money will come from to generate an economic recovery.

"The stock market's prolonged tumble has wiped out about $2 trillion in retirement savings over 15 months, a blow that could force workers to stay on the job longer than planned, tighten their wallets and possibly further stall an economy reliant on consumer spending, Congress' top budget analyst said Tuesday." (2)

Many investors are shocked to open their 401K, IRA and pension funds statements to see a tremendous loss inn their nest egg savings. What happened, they ask, dumbfounded.

A quick glance at the stock prices the majority of the investing class population holds amply illustrates the ugly side of the buy and hold strategy. Table 1.1 depicts 15 of the most widely held stocks in pension funds, mutual funds, institutional and investors portfolios. As an investor you have experienced the agony of opening up your monthly statement for the latest loss in your investment and pension fund portfolio. You have noticed how drastically your equity account has depreciated if you were holding any well publicized "sound" investment stocks including: National City Corporation (NCC), Morgan Stanley (MS), Fannie Mae (FNM), Freddie Mac (FRM), Wachovia Corp. (WB), General Electric Co. (GE), Apple Inc. (AAPL), Washington Mutual (WM), American International Group (AIG), MBIA (MBI), Ambac Financial Group (ABK), Citigroup (C), Lehman Brothers Holdings (LEHMQ), Merrill Lynch (MER), UBS (UBS), Bank of America Corp. (BAC), General Motors Corp. (GM), and Ford Motor Company (F).

No.	Stocks (ticker symbol)	52-Week High	52-Week low	52-Week change
1	National City Corporation (NCC)	$20.49 (11/30/07)	$1.25 (9/29/08)	-91.82%
2	Morgan Stanley (MS)	$55.39 (12/24/07)	$6.71 (10/10/08)	-79.86%
3	Fannie Mae (FNM)	$40.45 (12/31/07)	$0.30 (11/21/08)	-99.07%
4	Freddie Mac (FRE)	$37.18 (12/7/07)	$0.25 (9/17/08)	-98.45%
5	Wachovia Corp. (WB)	$45.43 (12/7/07)	$0.75 (9/29/08)	-89.94%
6	General Electric Co. (GE)	$38.67 (11/30/07)	$12.58 (11/20/08)	-62.76%
7	Apple Inc. (AAPL)	$202.96 (12/27/07)	$79.14 (11/21/08)	-51.86%
8	Ambac Financial Group (ABK)	$32.28 (12/10/07)	$0.76 (11/19/08)	-95.19%
9	Citigroup (C)	$35.29 (12/11/07)	$3.05 (11/21/08)	-88.11%
10	Lehman Brothers Holdings (LEHMQ)	$66.58 (2/01/07)	$0.02 (9/30/08)	-99.95%
11	Merrill Lynch (MER)	$63.11 (12/10/07)	$7.08 (11/21/08)	-84.42%
12	UBS (UBS)	$51.89 (12/10/07)	$8.33 (11/20/08)	-79.11%
13	Bank of America Corp. (BAC)	$47.00 (12/11/07)	$10.01 (11/21/08)	-73.42%
14	General Motors Corp. (GM)	$29.95 (11/30/07)	$1.70 (11/20/08)	-88.73%
15	Ford Motor Company (F)	$8.79 (4/24/08)	$1.01 (11/20/08)	-80.11%

Table 3.2 – This table lists the price changes for some of the widely held stocks by investors.

Please understand, however, that I don't propose market timing that intends to forecast market bottoms and tops. On the contrary, I propose timing with a proper trading method and system, on in which an investment expert can show you when you should buy or sell your investment for maximum profit potential. In other words, although no expert can predict the market's top or bottom—that would not be realistic or even practical—however, I can teach you under what market conditions you should buy or sell your investments to make the most profit. That strategy is indeed not only realistic, but also trustworthy.

None of this, of course, is meant to imply that you should not have a long-term plan for investing. In fact, long-term investment planning is an absolute must. Long-term planning, however, should not be confused with long-term investing. Let me clarify. *Long-term planning* typically corresponds to the buy-and-hold strategy and connotes taking a passive attitude toward your portfolio, complacently waiting for market "corrections" to take care of any problems with your stocks. The idea is that if you just wait long enough, you'll see improvement. In reality, of course, standing idly by waiting for things to get better is really no strategy at all. For instance, if the "check engine" light on your car went on, would you assume that if you waited it out, gave it enough time, that whatever problem your car was having would just take care of itself? Only if you want to destroy your engine! A smarter move would be to take corrective action at the first sign of serious problems—and that applies to your stock portfolio as well.

On the other hand, my definition of long-term planning is setting clearly definable and achievable goals for where you want to be financially down life's road, taking into account any changing financial circumstances you may face as your values and living situation change over the years; for example, you may marry, have children, buy a home, or change careers. Such goal-setting also involves a detailed assessment of your risk tolerance as well as your present financial situation. And then, once you've established these goals, you can devise the strategy that will most likely help you achieve them. The main point of this approach, though, is that you can be proactive and take charge of your own future for the long term. You don't have to simply wait (and hope) for conditions to improve based on nothing but shaky historical statistical analyses and, in large part, blind luck. That's a strategy that doesn't even work in Las Vegas.

3. Mutual funds. Another primary characteristic of the old paradigm is investors' heavy reliance on mutual funds. Traditionally, mutual funds have been considered the best option for many investors. These investment vehicles, however, came with hefty expenses and lower-than-market-average performance.

So why did the mutual funds industry grow larger than it could handle? Mainly because investors were told that mutual funds would provide diversification. What they were not told, however, was that most of funds were comprised of just a few major stocks. And most of them didn't learn about it until the recent stock market correction, when a majority of funds, which were basically holding only the stock of a few technology companies, went into the red—not exactly the diversification these investors had hoped for.

4. Slow to enter and exit. Using mutual funds as primary investment tools has another problem. For example, if you wanted to buy a mutual fund, you'd have to wait until the end of closing day and purchase it for the next day's opening price, missing potential good opportunities. Likewise, if you decided to exit a mutual fund or try to protect your hard-earned investment against market corrections and sell-off, you'd have to wait until the end of the day and get the closing price. In other words, in both entry and exit sticker prices, you were dealt the short end of the stick.

5. Hefty loads and fees. Mutual funds charge you a fee either to buy or sell them. In addition, some mutual funds advertised as no-load funds still charge hefty fees under Section 12-b, which allows for advertising expenses. Either way, you have to pay high fees. To justify such a large expense, your fund should gain high returns, but the majority of times, funds perform at less than the market average.

6. Taxes and taxes. When you invest in a mutual fund, you have to pay taxes on your return. That's fine if you're making a profit on them. But as incredible as it may seem, you also have to pay taxes if you have a losing year. Since your mutual fund managers had to buy and sell the holding stocks, you, as the stockholder, also have to carry the fund manger's burden. So even when your mutual fund has a negative return, you have to pay taxes on it. This is called capital gain distribution.

7. Inability to sell short or go long. It's important to understand the concept of short-selling (also called shorting), so do not be afraid of it. Armed with a proper understanding of it, you could yield much better returns. Shorting in finance and trading is selling a security without first owning it, for the purpose of repurchasing it later for a lower price. This could be very profitable if your analysis indicates a high probability that the security will fall and lose its value. For example, your market analysis indicates that ABC stock, priced at $50, could fall to $25 in the near future. You could short-sell it at current market price and then, as soon as it drops to the anticipated lower price, repurchase it, making a profit for $25. The market offers many great opportunities short-selling. However, your mutual fund managers may be unable to take advantage of them.

8. Heavy reliance on fundamental analysis. Fundamental analysis is a good method to gauge global investment trends. However, it's slow and doesn't reflect all of the dynamic price fluctuations. In today's fast-moving global economy, you need more agile and flexible analysis methods to decipher market information. This means understating and practicing technical analysis, which is mostly absent in the old paradigm.

9. Light portfolio monitoring. The tradition in the old paradigm is to look at your investment portfolio once a year. However, active monitoring of your investments can save you from losses that could make the difference between a winning portfolio and a losing one. And with today's high-speed mobility of information, you can access your portfolio and monitor its progress as often as necessary, rendering the old once-a-year practice useless.

10. Asset selection based merely on asset-specific risk. Many sophisticated theories and metrics can help you identify the risk associated with a security or asset: solvency, liquidity, profitability, interest risk, inflation risk, political risk, and more. However, any investment decision should factor in another aspect of risk: your personal tolerance for it. Ultimately, you are the one who has to decide whether to hold an asset in an adverse situation. The old investment paradigm has neglected this aspect of risk analysis, focusing on the assets rather than the investor.

Chapter 3 References

1. AARP 2002 Survey
2. Trejos, Nancy, *The Washington Post*, , October 8, 2008

Chapter 4:
Characteristics of the New
Investment Paradigm

Now that we've seen how things worked under the old paradigm of investing, we are in a much better position to examine the characteristics of the new investment paradigm. As you will soon realize, it's like the difference between night and day.

Online trading

In the old-paradigm environment, you had to call or visit your broker's office to trade stocks and investment holdings. Dealing with brokers in this way is not only unnecessarily time-consuming but can also be emotionally burdensome. If you've already been involved with a broker in this way, you know what I mean. For example, how many times have you put off making that phone call to sell your stock because you didn't want to hear another of your broker's sales pitches? Or had to leave countless messages for your broker, waiting for him to return your call according to his work schedule? And while you were waiting, your stock kept dropping, resulting in financial loss and regret, both of which can really take a toll on your peace of mind and even your health.

That's why the new investment paradigm has harnessed advanced technology and the Internet. Doing so has caused the speed of transactions to jump from tediously slow to lightning fast, and it has enabled investors to do what they wish with their own stocks, even in hectic markets. More specifically, under the new paradigm, you can place orders using an online trading platform provided by the brokerage houses buying and selling stocks and any other investment holdings in a matter of seconds, regardless of whether you're a professional or novice investor. What a huge difference this makes in the ease and speed with which you can conduct business.

High volume

Internet technology has not only made managing investments easier, enabling investors access their investment holdings and sell or buy them as often as they wish; it has also lowered related commission costs. The combination of these two benefits has led to a tremendous increase in trading. Figure 4.1 depicts this trading volume increase from 1996 to 2005.

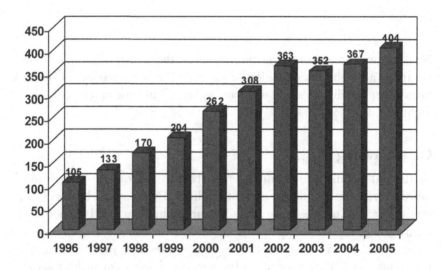

Figure 4.1. New York Stock Exchange volume shares traded in billions, from 1996 to 2005.

Flexible and active management

Under the new paradigm, investors no longer need to wait for the end of the year to make proper tactical changes in their asset allocations and holdings. Astute investors with technical-analysis knowledge and tools can adjust their portfolio's holdings—in response to either adverse market conditions or new promising opportunities—at any time of the year. And such flexibility results in their portfolio's maximum performance.

Exchange Traded Funds (ETFs)

Since the inception of the first ETF (SPDR by State Street Global Advisors in 1993), ETFs have continued to gain popularity and attract assets at a rapid pace. The contributing factors in ETF's popularity (ETFs are one of the favorite news kids on the investment block) are their low associated costs and expenses, flexibility, and tax efficiency. Let's review each of ETF's features more specifically.

1. Trading market basket or index with one stock. ETF is like a mutual fund in that it is comprised of many stocks but trades like a single stock. This enables investors to hold different market indexes as just one single stock. The most popular ETFs are currently SPY, or Spider, which represent Standard & Poor's 500 LargeCap Index; QQQQ, or Qs (pronounced cubes), which represents the NASDAQ 100 Technology Index; and D, or Diamond, which represents the Dow Jones 30 Industrial Stocks Index.

2. Intraday trading. Since ETFs are like stocks, you can trade them in intraday, meaning you don't have to wait until the end of the business day to buy or sell them. (If you recall, however, this is contrary to their counterparts, mutual funds.) In other words, you can buy and sell ETFs during market hours. This feature provides great flexibility for investors, enabling them to manage their investments even in adverse market conditions.

3. Short-selling. As discussed above and in the previous chapter, ETFs allow you to short-sell at the current price and then repurchasing at a lower price to turn a profit. And since ETFs are like single entities representing baskets of specific sector or market stocks, this could mean even greater profits for your investment dollars.

4. Low expense ratio. ETFs, in general, carry much lower costs and expense ratios than mutual funds. This feature helps investors to not only gain better returns on their investments, but also to save money. In fact, about 80 percent of the more expensive mutual funds are unable to match or beat the ETF's corresponding benchmarks. Here's just one example: Among mutual funds, the Vanguard 500 Index Fund is among the least expensive of the index funds. However, its expense is still 18 basis points, compared to its counterpart, Spider 500 ETF, which is only 11 basis points. In addition, Spider 500 ETF's cost is 40 percent lower than the most cited low-cost mutual fund in the Vanguard 500 Index Fund.

So although you'd need to pay a commission to buy or sell an ETF, as you would with other stocks, this lower expense ratio by itself should help you earn more money from your investment than the alternative.

5. Effective tool for diversification. To construct a winning portfolio you must diversify. By using ETFs, with their lower expense ratios, you can diversify more efficiently and hence maximize your portfolio return, even when you haven't invested a large amount of money.

There are hundreds of ETFs covering a vast array of market indexes that could be useful for diversification. For example, for major and more popular market indexes, there is Dow Jones, S&P, and NASDAQ. There are also many international ETFs that cover Europe, the Pacific Rim, Japan, Australia, and the U.K. There are also precious metals such as gold, oil and energy, real estates, and REITs. Some of the ETFs also pay dividends or are fixed income. I will review different types of ETFs in future chapters.

6. Tax efficiency. Another attractive feature of ETFs is their tax efficiency. This efficiency comes from less turnover as well as the special structure of ETFs. For example, investors trading large volumes could redeem their ETFs for a share of stocks, reducing tax implications for the large investors. Further, you can trade ETFs that don't pay dividends or significant capital gains distributions. We'll learn more about this feature in future chapters.

Wider asset class choices

Professionals continue inventing new and different securities for investors with specific needs. The resulting increase in asset class choices can help you choose investments that are more compatible with your risk tolerance and more suitable to your specific needs. And more suitable investments mean increased returns.

Willingness to risk for higher performance

It seems investors, primarily due to their desire to increase their incomes, have become more opportunistic, seeming to display an overall tendency to take more risk than investors of previous generations.

Now that we've reviewed the basic differences between the old and new paradigms of investing (summarized in Table 4.1), the challenge is to put all of that knowledge into practice to create a sound supplementary income through proper investment. In the next chapter, we'll learn the first step toward constructing a winning portfolio while setting proper investment goals.

Comparison: Old and New Investment Paradigms	
Old paradigm	**New paradigm**
Reliant on a broker to trade	Can trade online
Low trading volume	High trading volume
Buy-and-hold strategy used	Active short-term trading used
Mutual funds	Exchange Traded Funds (ETFs)
Few asset class choices	Wide asset class choices
Lower risk tolerance	Higher risk tolerance due to higher performance

Table 4.1. The main differences between the old and new investment paradigms

Chapter 5:

Your Investment Goals

Successful investing begins with setting investment goals. In fact, establishing financial objectives should be your first step toward not only investments but financial independence as well. In this section, we review the proper components of investment goals.

What are your investment goals? What financial wishes and dreams do you want to make come true? Here is your chance to map out your dreams. However, before you start thinking too much about your next vacation, dream house, or car, consider the following two basic goals:

1. Reduce your debt

According to a survey, 54 percent of Americans wish to be able to regularly pay for their bills and other financial obligations. Seventy-one percent of respondents, however, cited that their first financial goal was to get rid of their debt (1). Most of us know that dealing with any kind of debt can be stressful. But credit cards in particular are so stressful because they often carry high interest rates, accumulating interest faster than you can pay the minimum amount due.

For this reason, it is very easy to fall into the trap of credit cards. An open line of credit is, for many people, too much of a temptation to handle. They end up buying things that they don't really need and can't really afford. When the bill comes due, they scrape together only enough for the minimum payment, but the credit card company keeps adding interest and tacking on various fees (late fees, over-the-limit fees, etc.). Before long, the consumer owes far more on their purchases than they would have had they simply used cash.

2. Keep an emergency fund

Make it a top priority to establish a "rainy day" fund, one that could support you in the case of a lay-off or other emergency. Each of us tends to take our health, our job and financial stability, and our life in general for granted. However, with imminent lay-offs in many industries, and with the recent mortgage meltdown and financial crisis, it should be obvious that the wise need always to expect the unexpected. So if you haven't already, take the recent upheavals as a wake-up call and establish an emergency fund that can support your financial needs for at least three months. To figure out the minimum amount you'd need in your emergency fund, calculate your monthly expenses and then multiply that amount by three.

Once you've prioritized these two basic financial goals, it's time to set your objectives for investing. As you begin this process, remember to consider the following factors:

1. Your life stage. This factor often determines your overall attitude toward savings and your "emotional attitude" toward money in general. The following five life stages comprise sets of attitudes, values, concerns, and assumptions which may, or may not, pertain to you. If nothing else, they can be used as a spring board for your thinking about your own life situation.

- **High school and college (early to late teens)**

  You are just beginning to earn money, crossing over from the years of childhood in which you solely relied on your parents to pay expenses. If you are like the majority of high school and college students, you do not work full time, but you do earn some money. This is an ideal time to develop good financial habits and learn more about investing to help you with future needs such as paying off college loans, buying a car, and so on. In this age bracket, you can learn about investing through simple, set-term investments such as savings bonds and certificates of deposit. The returns will be small, but you will gain invaluable knowledge regarding how to invest responsibly and multiply your money

- **Family formation (early twenties to midthirties)**

  By this time in your life, you probably have a full-time job and have accumulated a number of assets such as cars, computers, furniture, etc. You may have also married. You likely use credit cards for vacations and other personal and family assets. You may be thinking of expanding your family and buying a house. As you increase your liabilities, however, you should be carefully considering your investments as well.

As you are still developing your personal and career life, you may be thinking retirement is too far away to worry about investing. Unfortunately, that attitude won't get you very far. Instead, see this time of life for what is: an era of great opportunity. Typically, you can sustain a greater risk tolerance than people in other age groups, so this is an ideal time to make your move, investing aggressively while you're still full of energy, promise, and potential.

- **Career development (midthirties to midfifties)**

  If you're at this stage of your life cycle, you are likely more concerned about developing your career life more fully. Your expenses are accumulating while your income is rising. Your main concerns could well be paying off your debts and mortgage, and saving for your children's college tuitions. You also need to think about investing in retirement and other important safety plans such as those for life insurance, disability, and so on.

  This is an ideal time to take an inventory of your financial life—where it stands now and where you want it to go. And as you reach the peak of your working years, you should have more money available to you for investing, especially if you've been resolutely determined to pay down your debt load.

- **Pre-retirement (midfifties to midsixties)**

  By this point, your investment goals should geared toward retirement and long-term care insurance. But of course, you may also be planning for that around-the-world cruise you've always wanted to take.

  At this critical juncture, you have one more opportunity to shore up your financial future. With your children grown, you might consider downsizing your home to free up even more money for additional investments. In short, you should be setting yourself up for a better, more stress-free lifestyle.

- **Retirement (midsixties and older)**

  In this stage, your main concern is to create a steady income with your investments, so that you can pay for your living expenses while enjoying your life. At last, you have reached the point where you can relax and enjoy the fruits of your many years of labor. And if you made proper investment choices through all those years, you can rest assured that, as the saying goes, "you will never outlive your money."

2. The span of your goals. One effective strategy for accomplishing your financial goals is to break them down into different periods, such as short-term, intermediate, and long-term. Short-term goals are considered those that can be accomplished within about one year; intermediate goals, between two to five years; and long-term goals, over six years. This one simple step will increase your chances for achieving these goals.

Table 5.1 provides examples of short-term, intermediate, and long-term financial goals for some of the different periods of life mentioned in the last section.

Personal situation	Short-term goals	Intermediate goals	Long-term goals
Single, midtwenties	Find a job or a better one	Pay off college loans	Create your investment portfolio
	Rent an apartment	Buy or upgrade your car	Buy a condominium
	Build an emergency fund	Start a retirement fund	Earn a master's degree
Married couple with children, late thirties	Increase your investment portfolio	Invest for children's college funds	Save for a down payment on a home or upgrade your home
	Upgrade your car and buy the second car	Take family vacations	
Married couple with children, late fifties	Train for possible career change	Shift your portfolio focus to income rather than growth	Downsize and possibly relocate for retirement

Table 5.1. Examples of financial goals at different stages of the life cycle

3. Financial goals are dynamic. Many people fall prey to the belief that their financial goals, as soon as they've been devised, are set forever. . However, financial goals should be dynamic. You should change them or adopt new ones based on new circumstances that may occur in your life.

For example, when you are single you set up certain financial goals that you most definitely will need to review when you get married. Or, let's say you buy a house.

Paying your mortgage on time (or even early) should become a priority. Also, keep in mind that you'll need additional income for basic maintenance and repairs on your home. In addition, you'll need to acquire and make regular payments for adequate homeowners insurance and set aside additional money for contingencies such as a leaky roof or a flooded basement that insurance would not cover. (And as an aside, be sure not to fall into the trap of using your home as an ATM. Lots of people did this during the "housing bubble" of the early twenty-first century, and later, piled under huge amounts of debt, came to regret it. While your equity in your home is an asset, it's one that should be held in reserve. Investing is a much smarter way to get the money that you need.)

Stated another way, your goals should define long- or short-term benchmarks on your journey toward financial independence and prosperity. Here are some examples of dynamic financial goals:

- Save to retire by age sixty-five with $500,000 in your account.
- Save for your MBA and graduate school tuition.
- Invest to earn $25,000 for a down payment on a first home or and upgraded one.
- Invest to earn enough to pay for your dream car.

Money can't bring you happiness, but it can help you reach it.

Before we proceed further with the discussion of investment goals, we should consider the emotional side of money. Money, by definition, is a tool used to purchase "tangible" goods or services for mainly intangible effects. With money we can secure a place to live, transportation to get around in, and other components of desirable lifestyles. However, the result is more than just owning and possessing tangible goods. When you really think about it, money has two dimensions: utility and psychological fulfillment. The psychology part is dominant, directly relating to our beliefs and attitudes toward money. And this dominance could be a primary reason why many will not set serious financial goals. On the one hand, they realize that without money, they cannot fulfill financial obligations and achieve independence. Yet, on the other hand, they may feel guilty and resentful about cultivating fortune, due to religious or cultural beliefs. Such cognitive dissonance creates internal conflict and distress, which naturally results in procrastination when it comes to financial planning. In fact, Americans seem to spend more time planning for parties and events than they do for their financial goals. Thus, the first true step in financial planning should be to examine your core beliefs about money and wealth, and to reconcile any views and beliefs that appear to conflict with your financial prosperity and happiness.

And what about "financial prosperity and happiness?" Am I saying that money can bring happiness? It's an age-old question, of course. But if we assume that happiness can be at least in part defined as a measure of satisfaction with life, some statistics indicate there may be a correlation. In a survey of people who made more than $75,000 a year, 56 percent stated they were "very satisfied" with life. But of people who make $25,000 a year, only 24 percent expressed the same (2). Table 5.2 below provides the complete results of the survey (3).

Annual income	Percentage of those "very satisfied" with life
$20,000 and less	22%
$20,000 to $49,900	30%
$50,000 to $89,900	42%
$90,000 and more	43%

Table 5.2. The relationship between family income and reported satisfaction with life (3)

This direct correlation between income and satisfaction with life may come in large part from the phenomenon that those with higher incomes don't spend as much time worrying about money. But, regardless of the reasons, the fact remains that if you do not resolve the negative feelings you may have toward money and wealth, you may inadvertently sabotage your effort to achieve financial independence.

Chapter 6:
SMART Goals and Attitudes

Before we tackle the proper mechanisms to achieve your goals, let's review another important way to set goals so that they are truly achievable: in short, your investment goals should be SMART.

S is for Specific

In my investment seminars, I ask attendees what their financial goals are. Here are some of the responses I continually receive:

- I want to be filthy rich so I don't ever worry about money again.
- I wish I was so rich that I could travel across the globe.
- I want to buy a good house in a decent neighborhood.
- I've always wanted to buy a new car.

To their disappointment, I can only tell them, "Yep, keep on dreaming." Because until you've worked toward your goals, they are just dreams and nothing more. That's not to say that highly accomplished and successful individuals do not dream like everybody else. Ask anyone, and you'll likely hear a laundry list of their wishes. The main difference between a dreamer and an achiever, however, is that the latter focuses his or her energy, somewhat like a laser beam, toward *specific* goals. By sharp contrast, his counterparts have no target for their energy, and so that energy just generally radiates, not going anywhere. Both have the same brightness in total, but one uses specific goals to help focus that light into an intense, effective tool; the other just sits wondering, letting the energy go to waste. In other words, the difference between financial success and failure is often caused by your ability to focus on specifics.

That's why any financial goals you set for yourself should be specific. As humans, we're naturally goal oriented, which means that when we set our goals properly, our subconscious minds look for opportunities to guide us to accomplishing them. Conversely, if our goals are not clear and specific, we act more like drunkards, wobbling around without a destination.

Let's apply this concept of making clear and specific goals to the four examples of objectives from the previous chapter.

Save to retire by age sixty-five with $500,000 in your account. This goal is very clear and specific. You know how much you should save for your retirement

Save for your MBA and graduate school tuition. But how much do you need$25,000 or $100,000? It'd be very difficult to achieve this goal since you don't have a clear and specific amount work toward. In other words, if you don't know how much you need to save, how can you save it?

Invest to earn $25,000 for a down payment on a first home or an upgraded one

Invest to earn enough to pay for your dream car. What does it mean to pay for your dream car? What is your dream car and how much would you need to pay for that particular model? Again, without specifics you are setting yourself up for failure and disappointment.

M is for Measurable

The second important component of the SMART model is *M*, which stands for Measurable. You should be able to measure your progress, and to do so you should have clear benchmarks. Benchmarks help you measure your progress toward achieving your objectives. To set benchmarks, you just divide the goal into smaller portions. For example, if your goal is to save $24,000 in two years for graduate school, that means you should save about $12,000 each year, or $1,000 per month, or $250 per week. By setting benchmarks in this way, you can measure how close you're getting each week to saving that $24,000. And in case you have a setback any particular week or month, your benchmark helps you know how much more you need to save the following week or month to make up for it. (And in this vein, you must remember that while working toward a benchmark, every choice you make either takes you one step closer to it or one step farther away.) Without any specific, measurable benchmarks, however, you could not ever expect to reach your goal. Before you knew it, your time would be up and you'd still be dreaming about getting that $24,000.

Consider the other goal above: saving $500,000 to retire on by the age of sixty-five. Well, if you're twenty-five now, you have forty years to work toward that goal. That means you'd need to save about $170 per month in an investment plan that pays 6.2 percent per year, not considering inflation and taxes. Or, you'd need to have about $22 of monthly savings in an account or portfolio that has an annual yield of 12.2 percent per year.

Do you see how it would be more doable to try to save $40 per month for forty years than to try to come up with $1,000,000 all at once? Breaking down your financial goals into benchmarks that are measurable makes accomplishing them not only more doable, but also motivates you more to take action by helping you not to feel overwhelmed by what may otherwise seem like giant-sized goals.

A is for Attainable

A is the third important element of the SMART model; to achieve your goals, they should be Attainable. Suppose you wish to save $1,000,000 by end of this month. Is that attainable? Do you see any possibility of it happening under your current financial condition?

Further, when it comes to investing goals in particular, note that while earning a high return on your investment might be attainable, it may not always be something you could be sure of. In other words, while it might be possible, it may not be probable. Here's an example. Suppose that in the next two years you want to buy a new house that requires a down payment of $100,000. But based on your finances, you can't save more than $200 per month. To achieve your goal, then, you must create an investment portfolio or find another investment vehicle that could yield a return of about 259 percent per year. Well, you get my point.

Investment goal needs to be not just attainable, but realistically so. Otherwise, it's just wishful thinking.

R is for Realistic

The *R* in SMART stands for Realistic. Yes, I know you'd like to make a million dollars overnight through some magical formula or investment plan. But is that realistic? Suppose one of my goals is to grow wings and fly anywhere I want. If you laughed loud enough at that statement, you know what I mean by being realistic.

T is for Timetable.

Any SMART goal must have a Timetable to be meaningful. In fact, any investment goal without a timetable would not even qualify as a goal by definition. That's because when you set a goal, your main objective in doing so is to achieve it. But if you don't know by when you want to achieve it, then you really don't have a goal. Putting a timetable on your investment goals shows you're serious about them. A timetable allows you to schedule your efforts and create a specific action plan through which you can achieve your goals step by step.

Your timetable should be specific, too; to retire at a "young age" is too vague. What is "young age" to you? If it's fifty-five, then you need figure out what type of financial lifestyle you'd need accordingly: the investment vehicle you'd need, for example, or the type of investing you'd need to consider along with its associated risks.

Let's apply this idea of having a timetable to our running examples:

- Save to retire by age sixty-five with $500,000 in your account.
- Save for your MBA and graduate school tuition.
- Invest to earn $25,000 for a down payment on a first home or an upgraded one.
- Invest to earn enough to pay for your dream car

Only the first investment goal has proper timetable and, as such, has far more potential to be accomplished than the rest of them.

Now, let's apply a timetable to a couple of these goals and see how that can help us determine what type of investing each goal would require to accumulate the stated amounts.

Investment goal and time horizon	At 6.2%, you'll need to invest …	At 12.2%, you'll need to invest …	At 16.9%, you'll need to invest …
Have $25,000 for a down payment on a home: 5 years	$356.48/ month	$304.47/ month	$267.89/ month
Have $500,000 in retirement fund: 40 years	$237.76/ month	$39.89/month	$8.56/ month
Have $1000,000 in retirement fund: 40 years	$475.52/ month	$79.78/month	$17.14/ month

Table 6.1. Monthly savings and related required rate of return to achieve investment goals, not considering taxes and inflation. (You can make similar calculations by using any of the investment calculation tools found on the author's Web site: http://www.winningedgesystem.net/WESI/invetment_goals. html)

The Triple-A Formula for success

Once you have identified and written down your financial goals, and made them SMART, you need to jump into the process of achieving them with a good formula for success: the Triple-A Formula. The three A's in this formula are: Attitude, Aptitude, and Attain. These three facets of the successful financial life are not things that we are born with, however; rather, we must carefully and deliberately cultivate them within ourselves.

Attitude: the right one is half of the battle

Successful investing requires a success-oriented attitude or mindset. Fortunately, attitude is mostly psychological, which means that through discipline, you can train your mind to think positively and logically in all money matters. I realize, of course, that setting goals and being disciplined are easier said than done. Yet, without a certain mindset, you are unlikely ever to achieve your goals.

To ensure you have the right attitude about your financial life, reflect on your thoughts and then make sure they align precisely with your goals. For example, you can't set out to have a good, solid retirement and then spend all of your time dreaming about buying luxury items, all the while neglecting your investment fund.

Second, be determined. Building the determination to meet your goals starts in small steps. For example, the first step is often just not postponing the creation of a portfolio any longer. If you're like most, you can think of a million excuses to put off starting. There's always something more "important" to do, some reason to put it off yet another day. But that procrastination is just evidence that you're not taking investing seriously. If you were, you'd be putting it ahead of almost everything else on your to-do list. Have you ever noticed that when you really want to do something, you somehow *find* the time to do it? In other words, you have to set your mind on the idea that investing is not only something that's very important in your life, but something that should be priority. Once you do that, you can get rid of that attitude of complaining and stop finding excuses. Instead, you will find yourself taking forward strides and seeking out new solutions. Nothing succeeds better than the fierce determination of a committed investor.

Aptitude: learning about proper investing

Aptitude is also primarily a function of learning. In this case, you need to educate yourself by reading everything you can lay your hands on that speaks to the topic of investing—beginning with this book.

But reading all of the right material and speaking with the appropriate people is still only half of it. The second half is using the knowledge you gain to properly execute your plan. After all, a plan is useless unless you have both the know-how and the will to carry it out.

Attain: begin investing

By taking concrete steps to get started, such as opening an automatic savings account, you can assure yourself that investing will be one of your highest priorities.

It's all up to you. Remember, dreams don't just become realities all by themselves. It takes hard work and determination. Lots of dreams end up shattered on the shores of best intentions. Why? Mostly because people let themselves become distracted. They allow other things to consume their time and end up leaving their dreams by the wayside. Thankfully, there is a solution: having a plan, taking decisive action on it, and not being satisfied until that plan is fully executed. Once you set your mind to following that course, failure becomes the only thing that is impossible.

Let's get started: write down your investment goals

Getting your goals in writing makes a big difference. It not only helps you to get better organized, but it's a great motivator as well. You'll be much less likely to stray from the path you've established if you frequently check your progress. Use the following worksheet to write down your financial and investment goals. It's a great way to remind yourself of your plans and to keep track of the steps you are taking to achieve them.

My Investment Goals Worksheet

Short-term goals (1 year or less)

Goals	Priority	Required savings	Target date

Intermediate goals (2–5 years)

Goals	Priority	Required savings	Target date

Long-term goals (6 years or more)

Goals	Priority	Required savings	Target date

Table 6.2. Investment goals worksheet

Chapter 6 References

1. Marion Asnes with Andy Borinstein and Douglas King, "The Changing Face Affluence," *Money*, September 27, 202, p. 42; as noted in *Personal Financial Planning*, Gitman and Joehnk, Thomson South-Western 2008.

2. 2004 Associated Press poll.

3. "Would You Be Happier If You Were Richer? A Focusing Illusion," by D. Kahneman, A. Krueger, D. Schkade, N. Schwarz and A. Stone, Science, June 2006.

Part II

Constructing Winning
Investment Portfolio

Chapter 7:

Understanding Risk

The sole purpose of any investment strategy is to make money. In that sense, investing, in a way, could be defined as a means for creating additional income on your principle.

To make money this way, however, you need to take some risk. Risk is an inherent part of forming any investment strategy. In this chapter, we review some of the major characteristics of risk and learn methods to minimize it while targeting a higher return for our investment.

One way to invest is to put a certain amount of money each month toward obtaining your financial goal. Let's say you want to create an emergency fund of $25,000 in the next five years. Table 7.1 depicts different monthly saving scenarios with corresponding rates of return.

Investment goal and time horizon	At 6.2%, you'll need to invest ...	At 12.2%, you'll need to invest ...	At 16.9%, you'll need to invest ...
Have $25,000 to create your emergency fund in 5 years	$356.48/ month	$304.47/ month	$267.89/ month

Table 7.1. Monthly savings and related required rate of return to achieve investment goals

According to Table 7.1, is it possible to reach your $25,000 goal by investing just $282 per month, not considering inflation and tax implications? Yes, under the right circumstances. However, you'd need to find an investment that has an annual rate of return of 16.9 percent. Is that attainable? Sure it is. But it would require you to be aggressive and take some high risk. Are you willing to do that? Your answer to this one question will help you identify your risk tolerance and shape the overall investment approach you take, so don't answer too quickly. First, analyze your goals to determine whether you indeed *need* to take risk to achieve them. And if you do, then it's time to answer the more subtle and important question: to what extent are you willing ?

Not all risk is created equal

Our economy is built, in large part, on investors who are willing to assume a certain amount of risk. In fact, risk is an inherent part of any investment that seeks to create returns. For every reward we seek, we need to venture to find the proper risk for it. Therefore, the higher the return you expect, the higher the risk you need to be willing to take.

That's not to say that you will always achieve a higher rate of return by taking a higher risk, however. Some risk is indeed unwarranted. Consider this example: you want to generate a 12 percent return on your investment. Treasury bills or bonds will likely result in only 3 to 5 percent per year, so you need to look at more risky assets such as stocks, commodities, or precious metals. To do so, however, does not mean just buying the most risky stock that comes along, presuming it will yield the best return. If that's all the strategy you put into it, the only thing you may gain is a loss. The lesson? Not all risk is created equal.

Risk-management strategies

To become a successful investor, you need not only identify your tolerance for risk, but also be able to manage it. The two go hand in hand: knowing your risk tolerance helps you to choose the most appropriate methods to managing it.

Later, we will talk more about your specific tolerance level, using what I call the Risk Tolerance Index, but first let's visit the different risk-management strategies you have available.

1. Risk avoidance. This may sound overly simplistic, but one way to deal with any risk is to avoid it. It might make sense in your personal situation to avoid any type of investment that carries a risk beyond what you can tolerate. And sometimes, depending on your life stage, you may want to avoid having any risky asset in your portfolio at all. When you live on a fixed income, for example, you should keep your assets in safe liquid instruments such as treasury bills and notes. Or, if you are at a stage in your life when you are stressed or under the weather, the best choice is to avoid even making a decision about a risky investment; your emotional state could lead you to making decisions that are against your better judgment

2. Risk reduction. As mentioned, to achieve higher returns, you need to take risk. However, you can devise methods to reduce that risk (which is different from entirely eliminating it). One such method is diversification. Diversification reduces your risk while increasing your potential return. (This method is discussed in future sections in more detail). Another method: placing protective stop orders. In the same way that installing a burglar alarm in your home can reduce the risk of robbery, placing these orders on your stocks can reduce your risk of taking a major tumble in the market. For example, you wish to buy a stock for $47 but you decide not to take any risk more than $2 for your stock. As soon as you purchased the stock, you should place a stop loss order to sell at $45. By doing so, you limit your risk to $2 for holding the your stock.

3. Risk transfer. Sometimes the most appropriate choice is to transfer your risk to someone else through contractual agreements. Naturally, your cost increases as you shift or transfer more risk. In addition, you may need to accept less of a return in exchange for your feeling more secure about your investment. Insurance, in essence, is a risk-transfer tool. You buy insurance for your car or home to shift the burden of loss to your insurance company. In finance, you can likewise transfer your risk by purchasing options in which you would be protected in a market crash. Purchasing such options may mean losing some of your return, but if you think of it as purchasing peace of mind, you may decide it's worth the cost.

4. Risk acceptance or retention. This method of dealing with risk doesn't provide any protection. You decide to buy some penny stocks with the understanding that you could lose your investment the next day, for example. Purchasing lottery tickets is another example: when you buy them, you accept the inherent risk of losing your initial investment. This risk-management method could be used when the cost of insuring against the risk is much higher than the initial investment or even the asset that you intend to protect. Of course, beware that any risk that is not avoided, protected, or transferred is retained by you.

4. More about risk

In simple terms, risk can be defined as the probability of losing one's resources. To begin a small business is a risk; since two out of three new businesses go under in their second year of operation, the entrepreneur who invested the necessary resources—such as time, energy, and money—could lose it all in this relatively short time. This is a risk that he should have been aware of and willing to take beforehand, however.

Likewise, you will need to calculate the amount of risk you are taking before you make the decision to invest. Suppose you invest $50 in a company's stock, and while you expect the price to appreciate to $60 by the end of year, you know it could also go as low as $25. That tells you that to achieve a 20 percent return on your stock, you'd need to be willing to risk losing 50 percent of your original investment value. Can you tolerate such stock risk? What if there is a 50 percent chance of gaining 20 percent, but only a 10 percent chance of losing 50 percent—now are you willing to take the risk and buy the stock? To answer this question, let's review the characteristics of risk

Traditionally in financial literature, risk is characterized—that is, it is defined and measured—in regard to assets; in other words, specific methods are used to measure the riskiness of particular investment vehicles, such as stocks, bonds, real estate, precious metals, and so on. What these traditional theories have neglected, however, is the role of the investor or investment manager as it relates to risk. Nonetheless, that role is important, since the investor or manager is the one executing the investment portfolio.

In other words, risk-management theories typically focus only on asset-specific risk. On the other hand, I propose a more comprehensive approach, one that is specific in regard to both assets and agents. In the next two chapters, I will discuss both of these risk-management components.

Chapter 8:
Asset Risk Factors

One way to measure the risk of an asset is to look at how much its price has vacillated in the past. (Higher fluctuations usually signify volatility and instability.) Such vacillation can be quantified by a mathematical concept called standard deviation.

Standard deviation

Standard deviation is term used to denote asset price changes over a period of time. The more volatile an asset price, the more risk it holds.

Suppose you buy a stock today for $45, and in the next few weeks it closes at $25 and then $40 and finally $55. How would you feel about such rapid price fluctuation over the course of just a few weeks? Let's assume the return for your stock is 22 percent, while its standard deviation is 12.5 percent. Now compare this stock with a stock your friend bought at $45 that only went down to $40, then up to $47, and finally to $55 in the same period. Your friend's stock experienced only a 6.24 percent standard deviation, while still earning the same return as you: 22 percent (see Table 8.1).

Period	Your stock	Holding-period return	Standard deviation	Your friend's stock	Holding-period return	Standard deviation
1	$45			$45		
2	$25	22%	12.5%	$40	22%	6.24%
3	$40			$47		
4	$55			$55		

Table 8.1. The hypothetical performance and standard deviations of two stocks in the same period

As indicated, because your standard deviation is higher than your friend's, your stock carries more risk.

In addition to using the standard deviation, or volatility, of an asset as a benchmark for risk, , all being equal, it can also be used as a rather simple and clean method to compare and contrast the risk levels of various assets.

That said, however, the method does have its flaws. Namely, because standard deviation measures price fluctuations, it therefore considers both upward and downward price movements as negative. In reality, though, that's not always the case.

Consider the two scenarios illustrated in Table 8.2. Let's say you are considering the purchase of one of the two stocks listed and you want to base your decision on how risky each stock is based on its standard deviation. Stock ABC exhibited the following price changes from Week 1 through Week 6: from $45 to $50, $48, $56, and $50. Stock XYZ, in the same period went from $45 to $40, $42, $34, $40 and $33. Mathematically, these two stocks show a standard deviation of about 4.6 percent. So according to that measure, there is no difference between the two stocks. In reality, however, ABC seems less risky by far than XYZ since ABC's price fluctuations has an upward bias. The conclusion: standard deviation is not a perfect barometer of risk and, therefore, will not be the proper tool to use in every situation.

Period	Stock ABC	Stock XYZ
Week 1	$45	$45
Week 2	$50	$40
Week 3	$48	$42
Week 4	$56	$34
Week 5	$50	$40
Week 6	$57	$33

Table 8.2. Risk measurement via standard deviation for two stocks: ABC and XYZ

Risk pyramid

As illustrated in Figure 8.1, the risk pyramid is composed of three layers: market risk (also known as systematic risk), diversifiable risk, and investors' risk tolerance. Understanding each component should help you identify and mange your investment risk. Let us begin with the first of these: systematic or market risk.

Figure 8.1. Pyramid of risk components

Market or systematic risk

Suppose after you buy your stock, the market experiences a sharp correction. Most likely, —even if the market correction had no relationship to your particular stock and even though you had no influence on the fluctuation— your asset, along with many others in the market, would experience a sharp price drop. This is called systematic risk.

Fortunately, you can manage this systematic, or market, risk by implementing the proper strategies. The old paradigm, in line with the buy-and-hold philosophy, recommends that you just stay put, in a sense, just to hope and pray that the market rebounds sooner rather than later. However, with dynamic price-timing strategies or system trading, you could make a meaningful difference between your return and those of others who just follow the buy-and-hold strategy. In other words, while they likely continue to lose money, you can take the bull by the horns and make the most out of the market correction, seizing it as an opportunity to increase the yields on your investments.

To present my case, let's glance over the monthly NASDAQ Composite Index in Figure 8.2. In March 2000, the index reached an all-time high at about 5,132. By October 2002, it sold off to make a low of 1,108.50. In other words, in just over two years, it lost about 78 percent of its value. Following the buy-and-hold strategy during this time would have meant just sitting there, taking it on the chin while your portfolio was ravished, losing over 70 percent of its value. Then, during the next four years, from October 2002 to October 2007, it moved up to 2,861.50, or about 44 percent.

As an investor, you don't need to go through all of these money-losing market corrections. Yet the majority of financial textbooks and other information still promote that old approach hands-down. Book after book, analysts and brokers continue to propagate the myth that the buy-and-hold strategy is the way to go. Why? Supposedly, they say, the investor doesn't have any other choice but to stomach market risk. But you do have another choice. I will teach you a time-proven strategy to manage your investments for optimum performance, allowing you to leave the old, failed "strategy" where it belongs: in the financial dustbin.

Figure 8.2. Monthly NASDAQ Composite Index

Just imagine being able to sell your holdings and stay in cash. Even better, imagine being able to short the market and later cover your short positions for a huge profit. Meanwhile, investors who'd listened to their advisors and brokers would be singing a sad investment song for years to come.

Fortunately, you don't have to imagine. As a new-paradigm investor, not only can you protect your investment against potential huge losses by using a price-timing or trading system, but you can also turn any sharp market drop-off to your advantage by selling short the market or related Exchange Traded Funds (ETFs).

Diversifiable or unsystematic risk

While systematic risk relates directly to market behavior, unsystematic risk—usually called diversifiable risk—relates to each specific asset. In other words, it relates to how financially sound a particular stock is? Let's review different parts of diversifiable risk.

Credit risk. When investing in a government or corporate bond, you should know whether the issuer has a high enough credit rating to pay you back in time. Why? Because the credit worthiness of an asset is determined by the credit worthiness of the issuer. The issuer's credit worthiness is measured by different rating agencies that look at the issuer's history. Naturally, a high credit rating poses less risk. At the same time, a highly rated bond pays less interest than one with a lower rating, since more investors are willing to work with issuers who have strong credit.

Liquidity risk. The longer it takes for you to sell an asset, the less liquid that asset is. Liquidity usually has an inverse relationship to risk; the less liquid an asset, the more risky it is, at least for a short time horizon. So depending on the liquidity of your various assets, you can have a portfolio that contains many different risk levels. Therefore, all else being equal. many investors prefer more liquid assets such as stocks or bonds, over illiquid ones

Inflation risk. Purchasing a $10 basket of goods today that, next year, would cost $12 represents an annual price increase of $2 or a 20 percent inflation rate. Inflation diminishes your purchasing power not only as it relates to goods, but also as it pertains to assets. For this reason, inflation can be interpreted as a risk. For example, if you make 10 percent on your investment but the inflation rate is 3 percent, excluding tax liabilities, you'd make only about 7 percent. To protect yourself from this risk, be sure that your asset's possible annual return is more than the annual rate of inflation.

International risk

- **Currency risk.** If you invest in international markets, you need to consider currency fluctuations as a risk, because an adverse exchange rate could decrease your returns. Suppose you purchase a great stock in one of the Middle Eastern countries and it goes up by 15 percent. Then when you decide to sell and pick up the profit, you realize that that country's currency has depreciated against that of your home country by 20 percent. Because of the currency fluctuations, not only didn't you make 15 percent, but in addition, you lost 5 percent! Now, you'll have to wait—either until your stock price goes up another 20 percent, so that when you liquidate you can get that 15 percent or until the exchange rate becomes more favorable still—that is, if it ever does (of course, there's no guarantee). And remember that the risk you're taking due to exchange rate fluctuations is *in addition* to the stock market risk in that country.

- **Political risk.** Foreign investing also carries political risk. A change in regime or a revolution, for example, could create volatility for your investment. Therefore, in foreign investing, we can use volatility as a good measure for asset-specific risk.

Using volatility to measure risk, however, is not restricted to foreign investing. In finance in general, we use an asset's standard deviation from its average rate of return as a measure of volatility.

But if volatility is such a risk to your investment portfolio, wouldn't it be wise just to reduce or avoid it? Yes and no. Risk and return are two sides of the same coin; as one is reduced, so is the other. So if you reduce your portfolio's volatility, you'd get less of a return, too.

One factor in investment success is learning how to reduce volatility while increasing return. We'll discuss more about this topic in future sections.

Chapter 9:

Investor Risk Tolerance

As mentioned, traditional risk-management theories typically focus only on asset-specific risk. However, new-paradigm investment takes a more comprehensive approach, measuring risk as it relates both to assets and the agent. The new paradigm recognizes that focusing on asset risk alone is not enough, because if five investors with five different risk profiles invest in the exact same asset, they will likely see five different performance levels, based on how each manages the investment.

Consider the following example. Many bought Google stock when it was first offered at $100 in August 2004. As of March 25, 2008, the stock had a closing price of about $450.78, and that was after reaching an all-time high of $734.89 on November 8, 2007. (See Figure 9.1.) Not all investors held on to reap the more than 400 percent increase return. Many sold, thinking it was overpriced or overbought and had little room to move higher. (Some had even said that Google analyst Safdar Rashti's call for the stock to reach $400 was ridiculous.)

This is a prime example of how the same stock, with the same risk, under the same market and economic conditions, saw many different levels of performance. That's because each investor behaves differently, based on risk profile and personality. Think about it: If you'd had stock in Google then, how would you have reacted? Would you have held it even until now or sold? Your answer to such questions would be based on your own risk tolerance.

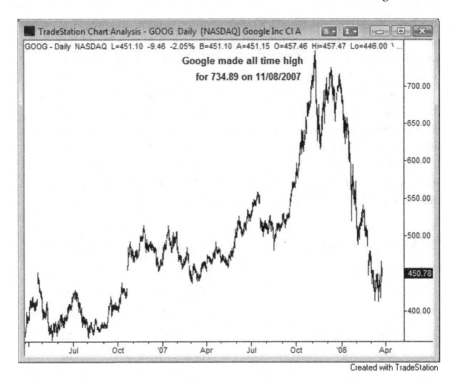

Figure 9.1. Despite Google's major stock variations since August 2004, when it was first offered on the trade floor, its initial price of $100 rose to an all-time high of $734.89 on November 8, 2007

Before going any further, I should explain that there is a distinct difference between *risk capacity* and *risk tolerance*. Risk capacity refers to your financial ability to endure risk. Risk tolerance, on the other hand, deals with your psychological behavior toward taking risks.

So how do we identify an investor's risk tolerance or profile? By considering the following attributes.

Income level. Your income level can have a major bearing no only on how much risk you can afford but also on how you perceive risk.

How you perceive any given situation affects your life in general. Consequently, the level of your reaction to risk investment could be predicted based on something called your *utility function*—the way in which you perceive different amounts of money being valuable to you.

Utility function, in turn, can relate to your discretionary income. Discretionary income as the money you have left after satisfying your fixed costs such as mortgage, insurance, car loans, food, and so on.

Now, let's say you have $50,000 of discretionary income. You might be able to afford investing in a risky stock, say, one that could lose up to $10,000, since losing $10,000 from a $50,000 discretionary income likely wouldn't affect the way you conduct your life.

According to a study by The Conference Board , 82 percent of all discretionary income is held by those earning $100,000 or more per year. Average discretionary income for this group is a little more than $62,000, which is nearly 3 times above the U.S. average of $21,657.

In summary, if your income level is $100,000 or more, you have a high risk tolerance. If between $60,000 and $100,000, your risk tolerance is medium. For incomes less than $60,000, a low risk tolerance is in order.

Risk tolerance mode	Income level	Scores
Conservative	0–25K	5
Moderately conservative	26K–40K	10
Moderate	41K–75K	15
Moderately aggressive	76K–100K	20
Aggressive	100K or higher	25

Table 9.1. Possible scores for different income levels

Age. A vast body of research indicates that as we age, our risk tolerance decreases. One reason for this relationship could be that as we age we feel there is less chance to make up for any losses or be protective toward our assets since as we get older we are more likely to have fixed or limited sources of income.

Risk tolerance mode	Age ranges	Scores
Conservative	70 and up	5
Moderately conservative	60–69	10
Moderate	50–59	15
Moderately aggressive	35–49	20
Aggressive	34 and younger	25

Table 9.2. Possible scores for different age ranges

Time horizon. As you devise your portfolio it is important to identify your time horizon. Research indicates that assets with high standard deviations—for example, stocks that tend to have a negative return for short intervals—could pose less risk if considered for the long run. So your intended time horizon should influence your risk tolerance. That is, the shorter your time horizon (or the less time you intend to be invested in an asset) the more conservative your investment strategy should be for that asset, and market volatility could pose potential loss. With a longer time horizon, you can afford a more aggressive, risky portfolio strategy, accepting assets with short-term volatility in your portfolio.

Risk tolerance mode	Time horizon	Scores
Conservative	1–5 years	5
Moderately conservative	6–10 years	10
Moderate	11–15 years	15
Moderately aggressive	16– 24 years	20
Aggressive	25 years and up	25

Table 9.3. Possible scores for different investment time horizons

Personality. One of the chief factors that determines your risk tolerance is your personality. Personality, which determines how you respond to an event, is composed of three major elements: roughly 25 percent upbringing, 25 percent personal experience, and 50 percent genetic disposition (1). To maximize your performance at any endeavor, including investing, you need to be able to act on what you know. That's why the root of any lackluster investment is not knowing or understanding yourself, your emotional standing on things, your tendencies, and your reactions; that lack of understanding can hinder you from acting appropriately or even acting at all, resulting in failure. As such, personality has to be part of your Risk Tolerance Index and reading.

Risk tolerance mode	Corresponding personality trait levels	Scores
Conservative	Very low	25
Moderately conservative	Low	20
Moderate	Medium	15
Moderately aggressive	High	10
Aggressive	Very high	5

Table 9.4. Possible scores for different personality traits

Going back to Figure 6.1, if you're like most investors who love high yields, you'd go with that 16.9 percent return for about $17 per month—essentially, less than one Starbucks coffee per day—to have $1,000,000 in forty years. But, do you have the stomach to accept the associated risk? What happens if one day you realize you've lost half your total investment? How would you handle it? The bottom line: know your risk tolerance.

The Risk Tolerance Index Test

To identify your RTI, take the following short quiz. Of course, there are also more detailed, accurate tests available, but this test should give you a good estimate of your risk tolerance (3).

	Check the box in the right hand column that corresponds to your answer.	A	B	C	D	E
Time	What's your intended time horizon for your investment? A. 1 to 5 years B. 6 to 10 years C. 11 to 15 years D. 16 to 24 years E. 25 years and up					
Age	What's your age? A. 70 years or older B. 60 to 69 years C. 50 to 59 years D. 35 to 49 years E. 34 or younger					
Income	What's your income level? A. $0 to $25,000 B. $26,000 to $40,000 C. $41,000 to $75,000 D. $76,000 to $99,000 E. $100,000 or higher					
	Total Score for Time, Age, and Income Factors Add up your scores in each column, using the following equations: A = 1, B = 2, C = 3, D = 4, E = 5 (e.g., if you have two *E*'s check marked, the total score for that column would be 10).					

Next to each scenario using the following equations SA = 1, A = 2, N = 3, **D = 4, and SD = 5, mark the abbreviation that best depicts how strongly you agree or disagree (i.e., based on how similarly you would respond to that hypothetical situation). The abbreviations stand for the following:** SD = Strongly Disagree, D = Disagree, N = Neutral, A = Agree, SA = Strongly Agree

	Personality	SA	A	N	D	SD
1	You were convinced your stock would go to $130 from the $100 you paid for it. However, as soon as it went up to $105, you sold and pocketed the profit.					
2	You sold your stock at a big loss. You buy another stock that you'd like to hold until you make up for your first loss.					
3	After you purchase a stock, you fear for the worst.					
4	Most of the time, you feel edgy and are easily bothered by things.					
5	You seem to lose your temper easily.					
6	A great return on your investment makes you ecstatic. Conversely, a loss makes you feel angry and sometimes even depressed.					
7	When you lose money on an investment because you've made a bad decision, you feel embarrassed and keep it to yourself.					
8	When you see the market is going up, you cannot resist the temptation to buy stocks.					
9	Your friends call you a spender rather than a saver.					
10	If the market sells off, you feel panicked.					
11	You usually feel blue.					
12	You have frequent mood swings.					
13	Your friends describe you as less than predictable.					

14	You're inclined to believe in luck .					
15	When someone cuts you off in traffic, you get angry and sometimes even want revenge.					
	Total Personality Score Add up your scores in each column, using the following equations: SA = 1, A = 2, N = 3, D = 4, and SD = 5. (e.g., if you have two SD's check marked, the total score for that column would be 10).					
	Total RTI Score Add your Total Personality Score to your Total Score for Time, Age, and Income Factors above.					

Table 9.5. RTI assessment

Write your total RTI score here: RTI =

Now, identify your risk tolerance by comparing your RTI with the scores in the following table.

Portfolio model	Risk Tolerance Index score	Risk Tolerance Index (RTI)	Asset or portfolio volatility (σ)
Conservative	18 or lower	Very low	5%
Moderately conservative	19–36	Low	7%
Moderate	37–54	Medium	9%
Moderately aggressive	55–72	High	11%
Aggressive	73 or higher	Very high	13%

Table 9.6. Risk-tolerance classifications based on total RTI test score

In the past two chapters, we reviewed risk components and their attributes. Table 9.7 summarizes what we went over about investment risk. Now, you have a better understating of risk, let's discuss how to minimize your risk while maximizing your return so that you can construct an investment portfolio that will help you achieve your goals.

Risk components		Attributes	Measure
Market or systematic risk		Market behavior	Volatility
Diversifiable or unsystematic risk	Asset-specific	- Credit risk - Liquidity risk - Inflation risk - Currency risk - International risk (currency exchange and political risk)	Standard deviation, volatility
Investor risk tolerance	Agent-specific	- Income level - Age - Time horizon - Personality traits	Risk Tolerance Index (RTI)

Table 9.7. Different attributes for each of the two components of risk

Chapter 9 References

1. Ralph L. Piedmont (1998), *The Revised NEO Personality Investory, Clinical and Research Applications,* (New York: Plenum Press, New York 1998). The following research are cited the referenced book; Bouchard & McGue, 1990; Hershverger, Plomin, & Pedersen, 1995; Plomin, Chipuer, & Loehlin, 1990.

2. Distribution of realized returns from 1926 to 2003 based on *Stocks, Bonds, Bills, and Inflation: Valuation Edition 2003 Yearbook* (Chicago: Ibbotson Associates, 2003).

3. Ned Gandevani, 2002, *How to Become a Successful Trader—The Trading Personality Profile: Your Key to Maximizing Your Profit with Any System*, Writers Club Press.

Chapter 10:
Building Your Investment Portfolio

While many don't consider themselves rich enough to talk or even think about constructing an investment portfolio, in reality, nearly everyone holds a portfolio of some type. Surprised? Consider, then, exactly what an investment portfolio is: a collection of valuable things and assets that you own. If you own your house, jewelry, cars, checking accounts, or any other valuable assets, you're holding an investment portfolio.

As discussed in the previous chapter, however, to own and manage a successful portfolio, you need to ensure that its risk is compatible with your risk tolerance, since, ultimately, that tolerance is the critical driver in your deciding when to hold or fold.

Think of it this way: expecting to achieve high performance without considering your risk tolerance is like endeavoring to climb to a mountain's summit without noting your physical ability; regardless of how strong your motivation to reach your financial goals, you will inevitably fail unless you devise a strategy that realistically considers your capabilities—in this case, your risk tolerance and financial standing. Simply put, you must construct a portfolio that is compatible with who you are.

In this chapter, we'll go over the necessary steps toward constructing a winning portfolio and then managing it, with minimum risk, for maximum return. To begin, let's briefly examine the types of assets.

Asset classes

Assets are economically valuable resources that are owned or controlled by an individual, company, country, or other legal entity. Assets are grouped by characteristics and behaviors into classes. By clustering them in this way, we can understand and use them more effectively. Although members of each asset class share general traits, they also differ in individual attributes such as volatility, dividend yield, etc. These individual differences dictate that each asset class be broken down into subclasses.

As a general rule, there are two types of assets: financial and real. Financial assets are claims to or ownership of real assets. Financial assets are divided into three primary asset classes: cash, bonds, and equity. Real assets include primarily real estate and properties, precious metals, energy, and agricultural commodities.

Now let's go through the main characteristics of each asset class—such as volatility, liquidity, historical performance and yield, and associated costs of ownership—so you'll know how to use them properly for a winning investment portfolio.

Financial assets

Cash. Cash is the most liquid and least risky asset. It allows you to purchase anything you wish and invest in any way you want. On the other hand, its value can easily deteriorate due to inflation. If you had $100 today and didn't invest any of it, with an annual inflation rate of 3 percent, your cash would be worth only $97 in a year. In other words, inflation—or losing your purchasing power—is an inherent risk in holding cash as an asset. Therefore, a cash-only portfolio comes with low returns and a high risk of inflation.

Subclasses of cash assets are savings accounts, checking accounts, money markets, treasury bills, certificates of deposit, commercial papers, bankers' acceptance, Eurodollars, and repos.

> **Savings accounts**: This is one of the most basic bank accounts. Deposits accumulate simple annual interest, usually at a fairly modest rate.
>
> **Checking accounts**: Similar to a savings account but usually with a smaller interest rate and more frequent withdrawals in the form of checks written against the account.
>
> **Money markets**: Publicly traded issues that may be collateralized by mortgages and mortgage-backed securities (MBSs).
>
> **Treasury bills**: Debt obligations of the U.S. Treasury that have maturities of one year or less. Maturities for so-called T-bills are usually 91 days, 182 days, or 52 weeks.

Certificates of deposit (CDs): Also called time deposits, these certificates are issued by a bank or thrift and indicate that a specified sum of money has been deposited. CDs include maturity dates up to five years as well as specified interest rates, and they can be issued in any denomination.

Commercial papers: Short-term unsecured promissory notes issued by a corporation. The maturity of a commercial paper is typically less than 270 days; the most common maturity range is up to 30 to 50 days.

Bankers' acceptance: A short-term credit investment created by a nonfinancial firm and guaranteed by a bank as to payment. Acceptances are traded at discounts in the secondary market. These instruments have been a popular investment for money market funds. They are commonly used in international transactions.

Eurodollars: Deposits held in foreign banks or foreign branches of American banks.

Repos: A repo is an agreement in which one party sells a security to another party and agrees to repurchase it on a specified date for a specified price.

Bonds. Bonds comprise the second asset class. Just as corporations need funds to implement their business plans, the government needs ways to finance public projects and services. One method that both companies and the U.S. government frequently use to garner such funds is to borrow from us, the consumers. Essentially, they do this by issuing "IOU contracts" called bonds. In fact, because government and corporations are net borrowers, while consumers are net savers, we can lend them our additional money and savings with interest.

Bonds are fixed-interest "loans" we give to the government or to a company for which we can be paid back in full—and with interest—by a specified date known as the maturity date. The credit worthiness of the issuer will determine the bond's interest rate; so, for instance, a company with a better credit history and reputation would pay less interest than a new business with a more aggressive growth plan and risky future. And of all entities who issue bonds, the U.S. government pays the least interest.

The bonds asset class includes the following subclasses: treasury notes and bonds, corporate bonds, municipal bonds, mortgage securities, federal agency debt, and international bonds. These subclasses are differentiated by the following investment grades: junk (high-yield), government or corporate, short-term, intermediate, long-term, domestic, foreign, or emerging markets.

Treasury bonds: Debt obligations of the U.S. Treasury that have maturities of 10 years or more.

Corporate bonds: Debt obligations issued by corporations that have higher interest rates (also called coupon rates) than U.S. government bonds.

Municipal bonds ("muni bonds"): Offered by state or local governments to pay for special projects such as highways or sewers. The interest that investors receive is often exempt from income taxes.

Mortgage securities: Securities backed by a pool of mortgage loans.

Federal agency debt: Fixed-income securities issued by government agencies (e.g., FNMA).

International bonds: Collectively, global bonds, Eurobonds, and foreign bonds. Figure 10.1 compares the annual return of international bonds, U.S. government long-term bills and treasury bills from 1923 to 2003.

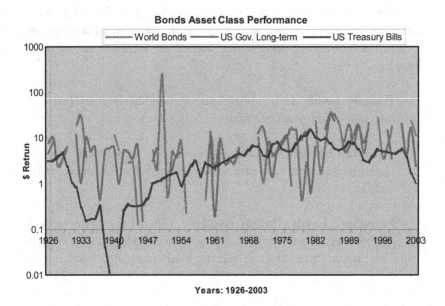

Figure 10.1. Historical bonds performance from 1926 to 2003, per annual return

As do all assets, bonds come with associated risks. Here's what you watch for.

1. Credit or default risk. It's rather easy for a corporation or municipality to issue bonds for its expansion or funding needs. It may not be so easy for them to pay back your money and interest in a timely matter. So, as an investor, you should be aware of the bond issuer's ability to do the latter.

Investigating a bond issuer's credit ratings and financial standings, however, requires a great deal of time and expertise—more than most of us have at our disposal. That's why there are major agencies that do such credit rating professionally. Using their ratings—and applying the knowledge that typically, the higher the rating, the less the interest (for instance, Zombie and Junk bonds pay the highest interest to attract investors away from the higher-grade bonds)—will help you make well-informed decisions about what bonds to add to your investment portfolio. Table 10.1 shows ratings from two professional ratings agencies.

2. Interest-rate risk. Another risk associated with bonds is fluctuations in the market interest rate. Although the coupon or discount rate of your bond is fixed until its maturity, whenever the market interest rate changes, the price of your bond changes inversely. In other words, an increase in the market interest rate would deteriorate the value of your bond. For example, let's say a bond has a face value of $1,000, pays 5 percent annually for 5 years, and is currently priced at $783.53. If the market interest rate goes up from 5 to 8 percent, your bond price goes down 5 percent to $680.58. The reason for this price depreciation: because after your interest rate goes up, investors could get a better interest rate elsewhere; therefore a lower price entices them to purchase your bond.

3. Prepayment risk. Sometimes the issuer of a bond may decide to pay off its debt due to a lower market interest rate. In such a situation, the issuer can refinance its project with a lower interest rate. This is all good for the bond issuer; however, the investor who holds that bond may lose a good fixed-income investment. If you invest in bonds, its prospectus should disclose all of the related risks, including tax-exempt features, in the bond provisions and documents. (Note that municipal bonds have a good chance of being exempt from state as well as federal income tax.)

4. Bond ratings. Bonds are rated based on the issuer's credit worthiness and projected financial standing. The ratings are then put into one of two main categories of quality: investment-grade bonds, which are at the high end of the quality scale, and junk bonds, which are of lower quality (i.e., have lower ratings). As such, investment bonds pay less interest than junk bonds.

The investment and junk bond categories are then broken down into various sublevels and assigned grades. Table 10.1 below exhibits grades appointed to each sublevel by the industry's best-known bond-rating agencies, Moody's and Standard & Poor's.

Bond quality	Moody's grades	S&P's grades
Investment Bonds		
Investment Bonds—Prime Grade	Aaa	AAA
Investment Bonds—High Grade	Aa, A	AA, A
Investment Bonds—Medium Grade	Bbb	BBB
Junk Bonds		
Junk Bonds	Ba, B	BB, B
Zombie Bonds	Caa, Ca, C	CCC, CC, C, D

Table 10.1. Grading system used by the two major rating agencies: Moody's and Standard & Poor's

Equity. A third asset class is equity, more commonly known as stocks. Equity, or stocks, represent your interest and ownership in a public company. When the company makes a profit, you receive your share of the profit as dividends. As such, buying equity is a great way to reap the benefits of a company's growth. Many good companies' stock prices have grown many fold since their initial offering price. Remember the example of Google? You could have owned its stock for as little as $100 in August 2004 and then gotten a more than 700 percent return on your investment by selling it in November 2007 when it moved to about a $747 high. But, remember, every good reward is accompanied by high risk, which means that any negative performance by the company could affect your investment's value as well; and in the worst-case scenario, a company could bankrupt, plummeting your investment to zero.

Many people misunderstand the stock market, focusing on cataclysmic events such as the 1929 crash that led to the Great Depression. These momentous occasions do, of course, affect the entire market. Yet, if you study the history of the stock market as a whole, you'll notice that it has built-in resiliency. Undervalued stocks usually come up sooner or later, and those that are overvalued eventually go down. Such market corrections overall—if not for one specific stock—are virtually inevitable.

There are two types of stock returns. The first is a capital return, which is when the amount of your stock increases from the price at which you bought it. The second kind of return is called a dividend, which is the payment a company makes every year to each of its shareholders.

When you buy stocks for your portfolio, you are exposing your total investment to an array of associated risks. Let's review those risks now.

Company or financial risk. The price of a stock offered by a public corporation could suffer from any of the following financial risks:

- **Profitability**: As an investor, you should look to buy either profitable companies upstarts with solid growth projection. Many dot-com upstarts, for example, began offering stocks while they were still in the red, and while most of them went under, a handful not only survived but also did very well—including Google. Nevertheless, profitability is the best measure of a company's solid financial position.

- **Liquidity**: When a company can consistently pay off its short-term (within one year) debt and financial obligations, it is said to be a liquid company. Often, even regardless of profitability, a company succeeds by way of proper financial management, which allows it to secure enough consistent cash flow to meet its short-term financial obligations. Why? Because even a profitable company cannot survive if it has a hard time managing its short-term cash flow needs.

- **Solvency**: A company's solvency is determined by its ability to pay long-term debts and financial obligations. High solvency signals success, while lack of solvency signals potential bankruptcy. Thus, when you a buy stock in a company that is not solvent, you expose your investment portfolio to potential loss.

Economic risk. When the economy is doing well, companies do likewise. However, as we all know, the economy goes through cycles, which can affect most, if not all, of a company's earnings.

In addition, while some companies do well as the economy grows, companies with defensive stocks do better as the economy shrinks. For example, companies such as bargain outlets that specialize in low-priced items would incur more risk in a strong, growing economy. That's because during good economic times, most people have enough money that they aren't focused so much on how to save. By contrast, companies that specialize in selling high-end products incur greater risk during tough economic times, especially during recessions, when consumers have less disposable income and are more reluctant to splurge on luxury items.

Market risk. The mere law of supply and demand creates an inherent risk in the market, especially in highly developed stock exchanges such as the United States'. Higher demand for any given stock or bond will drive its price upward; conversely, lower demand will drive the price downward.

But market risk is not just present in the stock exchange; take the real estate market, for example.

Of course, some market risk can be offset by protections such as insurance. The best such protection, however, comes from portfolio diversification. An old adage in the financial industry warns you not to put all of your eggs in one basket, which protects you from the inherent risk of holding only one single stock or any asset. In other words, the more you diversify, the better protected your investment will be. Imagine if you had put all of your money, for example, into Enron. When they went bust, so would all of your investment money. On the other hand, if your money had been properly spread out, or diversified, your risk would have been spread accordingly.

Another part of market risk that you should consider is "liquidity risk." Lack of liquidity occurs when there are few buyers for your stock when you decide to sell it, or few sellers when you decide to buy. Such situations force you to pay for a higher spread among any transactions you conduct; in other words, you end up buying at a price that is more than was quoted or selling for a price that was less than quoted.

Currency or exchange-rate risk. Before investing in foreign stocks, consider the exchange rate or currency risk you'd be exposed to. Suppose you invest in a European stock and the price appreciates from $20 to $25. At face value, it seems you made a $5 capital gain. However, suppose in that same period, the dollar appreciates against the Euro by 30 percent. If you sell your stock and convert the gain into dollars, you end up losing about 5 percent of your capital. Although international companies can provide alternatives against a slowdown in the U.S. economy, you should always consider the currency risk as you select stock for your portfolio.

Now that we've discussed the risks involved in equities, let's look at the various categories that stocks are often divided into: size (large cap, mid cap, and small cap), style (growth, blend, and value), and market type (domestic, foreign, and emerging).

Size

- **Large cap:** A stock with a high level of capitalization, usually at least $5 billion market value.

- **Mid cap**: A stock with capitalization usually between $1 billion and $5 billion.

- **Small cap**: A stock with a low level of capitalization, usually a total equity value of less than $500 million.

The above-mentioned categories for stock size have shown different returns which are depicted on table 10.2 and figure 10.2.

Distribution of Realized Returns from 1926 to 2002						
	Small-company stocks	Large-company stocks	Long-term corporate bonds	Long-term government bonds	U.S. Treasury bills	Inflation
Average return	16.9%	12.2%	6.2%	5.8%	3.8%	3.1%
Standard deviation	33.2%	20.5%	8.7%	9.4%	3.2%	4.4%
Excess return over T-Bonds	11.1%	6.4%	0.4%			

Table 10.2. The historical performance of different market indexes according Ibbotson Associates.

Style

- **Growth**: The common stock of a company that shows potential to earn more than the cost of its original investment.

- **Value**: Stocks that are priced lower than what their fundamentals (i.e. earnings, dividends, income, etc.) suggest are considered to be undervalued by value investors. Historically, value stocks have enjoyed higher average returns than growth stocks.

Market type

- **Domestic**: A nation's internal market, representing the mechanisms for issuing and trading securities of entities domiciled within that nation.

- **International**: Part of financial assets and securities market, representing foreign countries.

- **Emerging**: The financial market of a developing economy. For example, the recent emergence of BRIC (Brazil, Russia, India, and China) has proven a great investment choice for the new-paradigm investor.

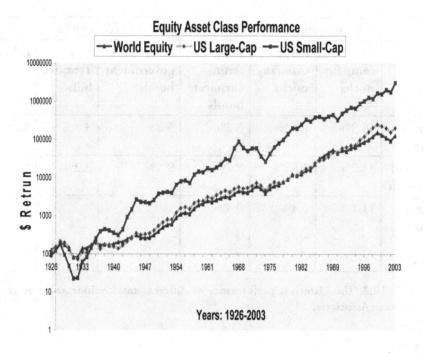

Figure 10.2. Equity asset class performance, 1926–2003; source: Ibbotson Associates.

Real assets

After financial assets, the other major type of asset is real assets. Real assets primarily include real estate (e.g, office buildings, shopping centers, resorts), precious metals (e.g., bullion gold, diamonds, platinum, silver), and energy and agricultural commodities (e.g., corn wheat, oil, natural gas).

The value of real assets can change with fluctuating economic conditions. These assets are also less liquid than financial assets since you likely couldn't sell them in a hurry if you wanted to. One good way to take advantage of their market growth, however, is to own related mutual funds and Exchange Traded Funds (ETFs). In recent years, for example, agricultural commodities and precious metals have seen a strong uptrend, so rather than owning the real asset—or, in other words, the actual commodities—you could own their ETFs and benefit from their huge upturn.

When it comes to real states and properties, their value depend mainly on the expertise and reputation of the property's management. For example, certain large commercial buildings are well managed, have solid occupants, come with long-term leases, and show excellent prospects for the future; investing in such properties would be considered a good risk

In this chapter we reviewed different characteristics of financial and real assets. To assemble a winning portfolio we need to learn about portfolio diversification. The next chapter covers the benefits and methods for diversifying your portfolio.

Chapter 11:
Diversify Your Investment Portfolio

To become a successful investor, you'll need to know not only how to earn profit but, more importantly, how to protect your portfolio against risk. As discussed previously, you can do this best by understanding and being able to manage two important types of risk: systematic and unsystematic. Systematic risk, if you'll remember, is associated with the market and thus with factors such as inflation, interest rates, exchange rates, and fluctuations in the economy. It's not company-specific; rather, all companies and then consumers, in turn, are affected by the market in general.

On the flip side, unsystematic or diversifiable risk relates to individual companies and, as such, is associated with factors such as business risk or credit risk. It includes any company- or asset-specific risk that can be prevented by better understanding the company's operations and finances, and implementing proper hedging and protection strategies. The main tool for hedging against such risk is diversification, a principle developed by Harry Markowitz, earning him the Nobel Prize for Economics in 1990.

Diversification does not mean owning different stocks of the same group, which likely share similar risk characteristics. Rather, it means investing in stocks that come from different industries and thus exhibit different risks. If you're holding a bunch of stocks in the housing sector, for example, any changes in the housing market would affect your portfolio's return. With the current mortgage meltdown, in particular, those returns would be negative. So despite your holding several stocks, since they are all in the same sector, your portfolio return gets hurt. Now let's say that along with your housing stocks, you're holding equity from the energy sector. In that case, your returns wouldn't be hurt as deeply, even as the housing stocks drop. In fact, you might have profited, since the energy sector has done very well in recent years. Thus, the simple but powerful concept of diversification.

While diversification cannot provide a guarantee against loss, it is an effective, practical way to minimize your risk by dividing your portfolio among different asset classes, sectors, and categories. It can also help you achieve better returns by allocating your assets among different securities and financial instruments.

Here's an example to illustrate the benefits of diversification. Suppose you and your friend each want to generate a high return on $100,000. Your friend feels more comfortable putting the money into a secure asset that pays only 6 percent annually. However, you wish to diversify your investment with the following results:

- $20K in a high-risk proposition, which is lost completely

- $20K in less-risky asset, which returns 0 percent, so you get only the original $20 K back

- $20K in a money market that grew 5 percent

- $20K in large-cap stocks, which returned 10 percent

- $20K in small-cap stocks, which gained 12 percent

Who do you think has a higher return? As Table 11.1 shows, despite some of the setbacks you experienced, your decision to diversify gained you a much better return—$962,800, compared to your friend's $429,187. How could that be, when you lost one-fifth of your total capital ($20,000) in your first investment, and on the second one-fifth, you made no money at all? Because you diversified, your overall performance was still about 2.24 times more than your friend's.

Investment A	Result A	Investment B	Result B
20K lost	$0		
20K in 0%	$20,000	100K in 6% safe investment vehicle	$429,187
20K in 5%	$67,727		
20K in 10%	$216,694		
20K in 15%	$658,379		
100K for 25 years in 5 different risky assets and instruments.	**$962,800**	100K for 25 years in a safe instrument.	**$429,187**

Table 11.1. Results of two $100,000 investments over 25 years show the benefit of diversification

Ned Gandevani, PhD

You can diversify via three general methods: vertical diversification, horizontal diversification, and cross diversification.

Vertical diversification. You diversify vertically when you focus on a single asset class such as equities, bonds, or physical (real) assets. Suppose rather than investing in bonds and fixed-income assets, you decide, at least for a few years, to focus your investment in stocks only. In order to diversify your stock portfolio, however, you'd need to invest in the stock of at least two different companies. That way, if one company's stock drops, but your others do better, you've reduced the overall loss on your portfolio. This is vertical diversification.

Although vertical diversification is more risky and requires more monitoring than the other types of diversification, it still makes your portfolio less risky than a nondiversified one. And depending on market conditions, it could even earn you handsome profits.

Horizontal diversification. When you diversify across different asset classes such as stocks, bonds, physical assets, and cash, your investment portfolio is horizontally diversified. This method of diversification creates a better trade-off between risk and return by choosing asset classes based on their historical performances and associated risks and then combining them into your portfolio. As such, this method allows you to minimize risk for a maximum return. In finance, this concept is called Modern Portfolio Theory, which we will cover in later sections.

Cross diversification. As mentioned, each asset class is divided into subclasses such as value, growth, large cap, mid cap, and small cap, as well as into sectors such as technology, retail, energy, and real estate. Suppose your investment includes stocks from energy sectors, technology, and large cap. This is cross diversifying.

One of the key advantages of this method is that you can spread out your investments over a broad spectrum. You can mix in stocks from diverse markets (say from both U.S. and emerging markets) and, within those markets, you can hold a combination of large-growth and small-growth investments. Moreover, you can target specific sectors such as real estate, energy, or agriculture, for investment. This method allows you to be creative in forming asset combinations from the widest array of options available.

Efficient diversification

If diversification is vital for successful investing, then how much diversification is enough? That is, if holding 10 stocks would reduce your risk, would holding 1,000 do it better? The overall conclusion of industry professionals is that there's a ceiling—a diversification limit that produces optimum results. According to a study of diversification using NYSE stocks, the standard deviation of a portfolio drops up to about 20 stocks, but after that point, the portfolio risk remains almost flat. The results indicate that a portfolio with more than 20 to 30 assets may not be much better than one with only 20 to 30 (1).

Correlation

The general consensus among financial professionals and academics is that a portfolio is truly diversified only when a distinct dissimilarity exists among its assets. In other words, to achieve real diversification, you need to minimize the *correlation* among your holdings.

Correlation refers to how closely two assets change in relation to each other, and it is measured by what's known as the *correlation coefficient*, denoted by ρ. The correlation coefficient of an asset ranges between -1 and $+1$. A correlation coefficient of exactly $+1$ means that as one stock moves either up or down, another stock or asset moves the same direction. Conversely, a -1 coefficient correlation denotes two stocks moving by equal amounts but in opposite directions. If the correlation coefficient is 0, the assets have no correlation; their movements are completely random. Therefore, choosing asset combinations that produce coefficients near zero can reduce your asset-specific risks.

In real life, you may not be able to find perfectly positive or negative correlated securities. However, the relative degree of correlation provides a practical guide for how to diversify.

Chapter 11 References

1. Meir Statman, "How Many Stocks Make a Diversified Portfolio?"
   Journal of Financial and Quantitative Analysis, 22, September 1987.

Chapter 12:

Asset Allocation

In order to diversify, you must use asset allocation. Asset allocation is a term that denotes what percentage of your total investment you've put into different assets. Suppose you have $10,000, of which you want to invest 50 percent in stocks, 30 percent in bonds, and the remaining 20 percent in cash. Table 12.1 depicts your asset allocation.

Asset	Allocation (%)	Amount
Stocks	50% of $10,000	$5,000
Bonds	30% of $10,000	$3,000
Cash	20% of $10,000	$2,000
Total	100%	$10,000

Table 12.1. Example of asset allocation for a $10,000 portfolio

Calculating risk

Now, let's consider another portfolio, which consists of only two assets: 60 percent large-company stocks and 40 percent long-term government bonds. Then let's say your stocks have provided 12.2 percent growth, while your bonds have grown 5.8 percent. How would you calculate your risk for such a portfolio?

In the same way that we use standard deviation to measure actual risk, we can use it to indicate potential risk when creating a portfolio. Although such a measure of risk is based on past data, which means it can't guarantee or even predict with high probability the exact future numbers, it can help create a framework from which to build a portfolio. To see what I mean, take a look at Table 12.2, which provides real historical data for the average return rates and standard deviations of different stocks and bonds. Then once you have a portfolio, you can monitor it and increase its potential return by learning how to use the Winning-Edge Investment System."

	Small-company stocks	Large-company stocks	Long-term corporate bonds	Long-term government bonds	U.S. Treasury bills	Inflation
Average return	16.9%	12.2%	6.2%	5.8%	3.8%	3.1%
Standard deviation	33.2%	20.5%	8.7%	9.4%	3.2%	4.4%

Table 12.2. Distribution of realized returns from 1926 to 2003 (1)

To calculate the standard deviation of any portfolio as a proxy of its riskiness, you'd use the following formula.

$$\sigma_p = (W_1^2 * \sigma_1^2 + W_2^2 * \sigma_2^2 + 2\ W_1 * W_2 * \sigma_1 * \sigma_2 * \rho)^{1/2} \qquad \text{(Formula 12.1)}$$

In which

σ_p = Portfolio standard deviation or risk

W_1 = Weight or portion of Asset 1

σ_1 = Standard deviation of Asset 1

W_2 = Weight or portion of Asset 2

σ_2 = Standard deviation of Asset 2

ρ_{12} = Correlation coefficient between the returns of the stocks and bonds

Now apply this equation to the above-mentioned portfolio (assuming the correlation coefficient is zero):

$$\sigma_p = (0.60 * 20.5 \text{ percent} + 0.40 * 9.4 \text{ percent})^2 = 12.78 \text{ percent}$$

In simple terms, you could expect to see about a 12.78 percent average vacillation in your portfolio.

Also, as you calculate risk, don't forget that your portfolio's risk is compatible with your risk tolerance. Then decide how to allocate your assets accordingly. (See table 9.6)

Calculating return

To calculate the expected performance of your portfolio, use the following formula:

$$E(r) = W_1 * E(r_1) + W_2 * E(r_2)$$
(Formula 12.2)

In which

$E(r)$ = Expected return for portfolio

W_1 = Weight or portion of Asset 1

$E(r_1)$ = Expected return for Asset 1

W_2 = Weight or portion of Asset 2

$E(r_2)$ = Expected return for Asset 2

By plugging in the information from our earlier example, we end up with the following:

$$E(r) = W_1 * E(r_1) + W_2 * E(r_2)$$

$$E(r) = 0.60 * 12.2 \text{ percent} + 0.40 * 6.2 \text{ percent}$$

$$E(r) = 0.0732 + 0.0186 = 0.098 \text{ or } 9.8 \text{ percent}$$

Now let's look at how the combination of projected return and risk can affect a particular portfolio. Table 12.3 depicts how performance and risk are affected by different allocation combinations of two risky assets: U.S. large-company stocks and long-term U.S. government bonds. Depending on your risk tolerance, one of the portfolios may suit your appetite better, while one may make you more uncomfortable. Conversely, your Risk Tolerance Index (RTI) should guide you to select a portfolio which has similar standard deviation as your RTI. According to Table 9.6, a portfolio with 12.78 percent standard deviation corresponds to a high score for RTI, 73 or higher, and Aggressive portfolio model.

For each asset-allocation combination, Table 12.3 shows the return-per-unit risk, which is, as you might imagine, how much of a return you should expect for each unit of risk you take. The table also depicts what's called the reward-to-variability (or risk) ratio. In order to understand how the reward-to-variability ratio is calculated, however, you must first understand what's called a risk premium.

Returns from risky assets such as long-term bonds or large-company stocks should be higher than those from risk-free assets, such as CDs or treasury bills, which pay only about 3 percent. (Otherwise, why would you invest in them in the first place?) The risk premium is the difference between a risky asset return and a risk-free return. Risk premium can be expressed as the following formula, in which a risky return is denoted by r and a low-risk return is denoted by r_f

Risk Premium (R) = $r - r_f$ (Formula 12.3)

Therefore, the risk premium of large-capital stocks, if the risk-free return is 3 percent, would be expressed as follows:

12.2 – 3 = 9.2 percent.

Now, we can understand the last column in Figure 12.2, which records the reward-to-variability ratio. The reward-to-variability ratio is the risk premium over the standard deviation. You'll notice that the shaded rows have the highest reward-to-variability (or risk) ratio, indicating that the best performance with respect to risk comes via 30 percent and 70 percent allocations, or 40 percent and 60 percent allocations for stocks and bonds respectively. For the same rows, return-per-unit risk is a bit higher for the 30 percent and 70 percent allocations than for the 40 percent and 60 percent allocations. Therefore, the 70/30 asset allocation configuration would likely yield the best performance with the lowest relative risk.

Stocks, percent of allocation	Bonds, percent of allocation	Portfolio return	Portfolio standard deviation	Return-per-unit risk	Reward-to-variability ratio
0	100	5.8	8.7	0.67	0.32
10	90	6.44	8.09	0.80	0.43
20	80	7.08	8.08	0.88	0.51
30	70	7.72	8.66	0.89	0.55
40	60	8.36	9.72	0.86	0.55
50	50	9	11.13	0.81	0.54
60	40	9.64	12.78	0.75	0.52
70	30	10.28	14.59	0.70	0.50
80	20	10.92	16.49	0.66	0.48
90	10	11.56	18.47	0.63	0.46
100	0	12.2	20.50	0.60	0.45

Table 12.3. The expected performance, standard deviation, and reward-to-variability ratio for a portfolio with various asset allocations of two risky assets: stocks and bonds

In the next chapters, we begin to learn about Exchange Traded Funds and how we can use them as a vehicle to reach your portfolio's maximum performance.

Chapter 12 References

1. Based on *Stocks, Bonds, Bills, and Inflation: Valuation Edition 2003 Yearbook*, Chicago, Ibbotson Associates, 2003.

Chapter 13:

ETFs for Your Investment Portfolio

In the previous section, we discussed constructing an investment portfolio by considering different asset classes such as cash, bonds, equity, and diversification. In this chapter, I'll explore Exchange Traded Funds (ETFs) as effective tools for achieving better performance.

Investing in the stock market can be a very complex undertaking. Yes, if you do your homework, you might make a significant profit. Of course, there's also the possibility of losing a large part of your portfolio. And if you are not a professional in the field, the odds are not good that you'll pick winning stocks.

That is what makes ETFs so attractive. They keep you from spending countless hours of guesswork trying to pick the right stocks.

An ETF is type of mutual fund that trades as a listed security on one of the stock exchanges. Up to now, all ETFs have been created as index funds, set up to match the performance of a market segment. An ETF is an index which is a collection of securities such as stocks, bonds, or futures but is traded intraday like a stock during market hours. ETFs provide the professional money mangmen6t of traditional mutual funds but at much lower cost and trading flexibility of a stock. The biggest and oldest ETFs are based on S&P 500 and are known as Spiders (SPDRs). But the most actively stock in the world is the NAADAQ 100 ETF known as Qubes. In addition Diamonds based on Dow Jones Industrial Average and many other ETFs based on international markets such as Japan, China, Russia, Brazil, Australia and many other indexes tracking different market segments and sectors. The nest asset value or price of ETFs are set as fraction of the underlying index value at any given time. For example, if S&P 500 index is at 925.80. The Spider (ticker symbol SPY) is priced at 92.60 or about 1/10 of the index value. Like wise if Dow Jones Industrial Average is 9034.69, the corresponding ETF, Diamond (ticker symbol DIA) trades at 90.35 or about 1/100 of the index value.

ETFs offer an advantage over actively managed funds. In actively managed funds, mangers decide on type of securities and their portions in the portfolios based on their own unique strategies. Despite hefty fees they charge, 80 percent of time actively traded funds perform less than broad market indexes. Since ETFs track the underlying indexes do not implement any market timing strategies.

In addition, actively managed funds are expensive to run, as fund managers, analysts, traders, and numerous other experts need to be paid. Costs associated with index funds, therefore, are much lower. ETFs, which represent passive index funds, are low-cost investment vehicles, in part because their expenses are spread around more efficiently than, for example, no-load mutual funds. For that reason, including ETFs in your portfolio can help you achieve better return with relatively less cost.

ETFs are new investment vehicles and an important component of the new-investment paradigm matrix. They are increasingly popular across the globe because they have a low cost, are highly diversified, and are easily traded. The number of ETFs increased by nearly 50 percent in 2006 alone, and there are now more than a half of a trillion dollars invested in 800 ETFs around the world. The United States has by far the largest market for ETFs, with over 70 percent of its global assets. The European market has seen impressive growth as well, with assets increasing by over 60 percent to nearly USD90bn in 2006 (1).

The proper use of ETFs is an important component of the new-investment paradigm. In the following sections, I show you how to select an ETF for your portfolio and later, how to manage them profitably.

ETF history

The Philadelphia Stock Exchange was the birthplace of the first U.S. ETF, in 1989. Europe made them available in 1999. Originally seen as traditional index funds, a cluster of traded securities tracking a sector, the concept of the ETF evolved by 2008 when the U.S. Securities and Exchange Commission (SEC) authorized the creation of actively managed ETFs.

In recent years, ETFs have become more customized, tailored to an increasingly specific array of regions, sectors, commodities, bonds, futures, and other asset classes. As of February 2008, the United States had a total of 634 ETFs, representing $559 billion in assets, a $126 billion increase over the previous twelve months.

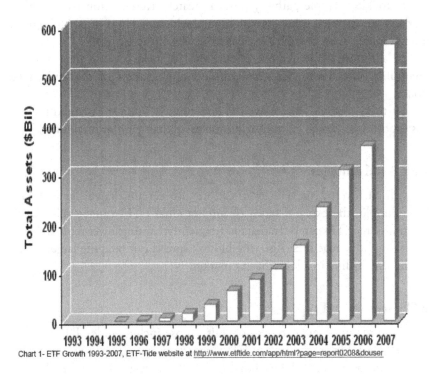

Chart 1- ETF Growth 1993-2007, ETF-Tide website at http://www.etftide.com/app/html?page=report0208&douser

Figure 13.1. ETF growth, 1993–2007 (2)

ETF advantages

A unique set of advantages makes ETFs attractive. They offer broad diversification with just one trade. They have liquidity because they are traded on the stock market and they are not constrained by the trading restrictions that impose limitations upon mutual funds. As an investor you should be able to recognize the strong appeal of ETFs. They could help you benefit from the recent phenomenal growth of oil, energy, precious metals, and commodities.

ETFs combine the best features of both mutual funds and individual stocks. For example, they offer the broad diversification of mutual funds, as well as the ability to track a benchmark and to target specific sectors and segments.

Since they can be traded at any time during market hours, ETFs are highly liquid compared to index mutual funds. They also have better valuation, since they can be traded in the secondary markets and offer trading options such as selling short, placing stop-loss or limit orders, and buying on margin.

They provide a simple pathway toward greater diversification and open up market segments that otherwise might not be included in your portfolio (e.g., international stocks or stocks in diverse sectors or industries).

In addition, ETFs remove a great deal of risk, because they generate premiums only when there is significant appreciation of the underlying stocks.

Further, dividends are reinvested immediately in most cases and there is less exposure to capital gains distribution taxes than with mutual funds.

ETF disadvantages

As with all investment vehicles, there are also certain drawbacks to ETFs. For example, the expense ratios of international ETFs can be substantial. Furthermore, ETFs can be traded too frequently, causing lower returns due to mounting brokerage fees. Also, the bid-ask spread can be quite large, which can be like trading in a less efficient market.

ETFs sectors and types

There are many different types of ETFs. Those include index ETFs, sector ETFs, style ETFs, commodities ETFs, international ETFs, currency ETFs, inverse and bear market ETFs, bond ETFs, and actively managed ETFs.

Index ETFs

These types of ETFs offer investors to invest in major market indexes like S&P 500, Russell 2000, and Dow Jones Industrial.
Examples:
iShares S&P 500 Index (IVV), iShares Russell 2000 Index (IWM), PowerShares QQQ Trust, Series 1 (QQQQ)

Sector ETFs

ETFs provide opportunities to invest in different sectors such as Basic Materials, Consumer Discretionary, Consumer Staples, Energy, Financials, Healthcare, Industrials, Technology, Telecom, Transportation, and Utilities. For example if you decide to expose your portfolio to international markets, you could use iShare MSCI ex US or iShare S&P Asia 50 ETFs.

Basic Materials – Those stocks that primarily deal with raw material for production and construction are categorized under basic materials. This category of stocks includes the mining and refining of industrial metals like steel, copper, gold, and platinum, forestry products and chemical produces. Consequently, this sector is sensitive to changes in economy and business cycles since it is largely a demand driven sector.

Consumer Discretionary – This category of stocks that primarily sell produces and services to consumers which are not necessities. This sector includes industries like automobiles, high-end clothing, restaurants, hotels and luxury goods. Since companies in this category deal with discretionary goods it's generally sensitive to economic changes and business cycles.

Consumer Staples – This sector refers to those companies that provide and produce consumer staples like food, beverages, household products, prescriptions, and tobacco. This sector is less sensitive to economic changes and business cycles.

Energy – This sector is comprised of stocks that engage in the exploration, production, refining, transportation, and marketing of oil, gas products, and coal. This sector could be sensitive to economic changes and business cycles.

Financials – This sector includes banks, insurance, investments, real-estate investment trusts, real estate, and savings and loans.

Healthcare – This category is comprised of stocks in the provision, distribution, and consumption of health care services and products. This sector includes hospital management firms, health maintenance organizations (HMOs), biomedical and biotechnology companies. This category is considered to be defensive since the products and services are necessary and less sensitive to business cycles and economic conditions.

Industrials – This category enlists companies in agriculture, construction, fisheries, forestry, and manufacturing. This sector is called cyclical since it is sensitive to business cycles and economics conditions

Technology – This sector encompasses companies from several areas including aerospace, business data processing, computer leasing, electrical equipment, specialized machinery, and precision instruments.

Telecom – This category of stocks deal with telecommunications technology, services and products.

Transportation – This sector deals with companies whose primary business is transporting people and goods from one physical location to another. This sectors includes mainly trucking companies, cargo train and airplanes, ships and barges.

Utilities – This category of companies involve in production, delivery and services of utilities to other companies and consumers.

Style ETFs

These kinds of ETFs allow investors to invest in companies by the size of companies and their objectives towards growth or value. For example, Spider (ticker symbol SPY) which tracks S&P 500 index is a large-cap index.
Examples:
S&P 500 Pure Value (RPV), S&P 500 Pure Growth (RPG), S&P MidCap 400 Pure Value (RFV), S&P MidCap 400 Pure Growth (RFG). S&P SmallCap 600 Pure Value (RZV), and S&P SmallCap Pure Growth (RZG)

Commodities ETFs

These ETFs let you invest in physical commodities such as natural resources, basic materials, and agricultural products. Investing in commodities ETFs provides your portfolio exposed growing demand for agricultural products, energy, precious metals and more.
Examples:
streetTRACKS Gold Shares (GLD), iShares COMEX Gold Trust (IAU), iPath Dow Jones-AIG Commodity Index (DJP).

International ETFs

Investing in international market could be an effective method to diversify your portfolio. International ETFs lets you do so without the hassles of dealing foreign stocks exchanges and currency conversions. International ETFs are especially useful if you're trying to gain exposure to smaller markets that would otherwise be costly or prohibitive to access on your own
Examples:
iShares Belgium Index (EWK) which tracks the MSCI Belgium Index. iShares Mexico (EWW), iShares FTSE/Xinhua 25 (FXI), Singapore (EWS), Malaysia (EWM), Taiwan (EWT), iShares S&P Europe 350 (IEV).

Currency ETFs

If you like to participate in the recent foreign exchange market explosion, using currency ETFs is an effective way. Since 2005, currency ETFs have offered investors to participate in currency market.
Examples:
CurrencyShares Euro Trust (FXE), and CurrencyShares Japanese Yen Trust (FXY).

Inverse and bear market ETFs

Based on your analysis, if you conclude stock market could sell off and drop lower, then you could use inverse ETFs to short sell the market. These ETFs are good way to ease the pain of declining your portfolio value in bear markets individual stocks or indexes.
Examples:
Short QQQ (PSQ), Short Dow 30 (DOG), and Short S&P 500 (SH).

Bond ETFs

An effective method to diversify your portfolio is to allocate part of it to bonds. These ETFs are great vehicles if you look for fixed income and provide broad exposures to U.S. Treasury and corporate bonds.
Examples:
iShares, issued by Barclays Global Investors (BGI), iShares Lehman 1-3 Year Treasury (SHY); iShares Lehman 7-10 Year Treasury (IEF); and iShares Lehman 20+ Year Treasury (TLT). iShares Lehman TIPS Bond (TIP), which invests in treasuries that are inflation-protected.

Actively managed ETFs

These types of ETFs are like their counter part mutual funds with higher expense and most probably lower returns. My recommendation is to stay away from these ETFs since they are counter productive to the main ideas of ETFs.

ETF sponsors

Table 13.1 lists the top ten sponsors who issue ETFs. Some of them, such as WisdomTree, take a fundamental approach like the dividend and cash flow approach in constructing its ETFs. Others like Rydex and ProFunds issue leverage and inverse ETFs.

	Sponsors	ETFs
	Barclays Global Investors	iShares
	State Street Global Advisors	TRACKS and SPDRs
	Vanguard Group	VIPERs
	Rydex	Rydex ETFs
	Merrill Lynch	HOLDRSs
	PowerShares	PowerShares ETFs and BLDRS
	Deutsche Bank	PowerShares DB commodity- and currency-based ETFs
	WisdomTree	WisdomTree ETFs— fundamentally weighted
	ProFunds	ProShares—inverse and leveraged ETFs.
	RevenueShares	Revenue-weighted ETFs

Table 13.1. Major sponsors of ETFs

Chapter 13 References

1. Nik Bienkowski, head of listings and research for ETF Securities, 2007

2. ETF-Tide Web site at http://www.etftide.com/app/html?page= report0208&douser

Chapter 14:
How to Choose ETFs for Your Portfolio

The assets you select for you portfolio can affect its performance. When selecting assets among ETFs, use the following criteria:

Size. ETFs representing small-cap companies could outperform large-cap ETFs. This is primarily because small companies have historically outperformed their counterpart large-capitalized companies. You can use Yahoo! to screen ETFs based on size: http://finance.yahoo.com/etf/browser/op

Price-to-book value. ETFs for stocks with low price-to-book value (P/B) may outperform ETFs for growth companies. Historically, low-P/B stocks tend to outperform growth stocks. Growth companies tend to be start-ups so their stock prices are relatively expensive, considering their book-to-market ratio relative to their book value and earnings. Both size and value are factors that researchers Fama and French showed to outperform the large size and growth stocks.

Price-to-earning value. Another factor you should consider in selecting ETFs for your portfolio is low price-to-earning (P/E) ratio. A body of research reveals that low P/E-ratio stocks tend to generate higher returns than stocks with high P/E. In that vein, ETFs representing low-P/E stocks should do better than ETFs for stocks with higher P/E. You can use Yahoo! Finance's prebuilt screen to browse for ETF's by P/E: http://finance.yahoo.com/etf/browser/hl?c=0&k=6&f=0&cs=1&ce=20&o=a

Beta coefficient. Beta coefficient is a measure of an ETF's volatility and risk with respect to its corresponding benchmark and index. The higher an ETF's beta, the more volatile it's been relative to its benchmark. When an ETF is more volatile than the benchmark index, its beta is greater than 1.0; if less volatile, its beta will be less than 1.0.

Keep in mind, of course, that an ETF's beta is only helpful when it is calculated against a relevant benchmark. If it is calculated against an inappropriate benchmark, its beta is meaningless.

Alpha. Alpha is another measurement of ETF performance, usually falling about a percentage above or below its beta. Positive alpha means an ETF performed greater than its beta suggested it would, while negative alpha means the ETF underperformed. So a 1.3 alpha indicates an ETF that outperformed its beta prediction by 1.3 percent. Thus, if you decided to have an ETF representing a small cap, you'd pick the one from the list of small-cap-only ETFs with the highest alpha.

R-squared. Another useful criterion for selecting an ETF is its R-squared: a statistical measure that denotes the percentage of an ETF's return related to its underlying benchmark performance. For example, the benchmark for a fixed-income ETF is the T-bill.

R-squared value ranges from 0 to 100. An ETF with an R-squared between 85 and 100 denotes performance explained mainly by its benchmark index. Conversely, a low R-squared—70 or less—does not reflect the benchmark. Since you select an ETF based on the index it represents, it's important to choose ones with high R-squared. Any departure from this guideline may lead unaccounted variables into your portfolio and cause unexpected performance. Further, when considering the beta of an ETF, you should note its R-squared, since the beta of a low R-squared ETF is meaningless. Conversely, a beta of less than 1.0 for a high R-squared ETF could mean a higher risk-adjusted return.

The above-mentioned factors are often provided by a sponsor with any ETF listing or available on the Internet at places such as the Yahoo! Finance Web site.

After narrowing down your ETF selections based on the above criteria, use the following factors to help you finalize your decision.

Ratio expenses. Compared to other asset holders, ETF investors often enjoy lower expenses as well as tax advantages. Mutual fund shareholders, for example, often have to pay capital gains taxes when fund managers move shares around. While this happens with ETFs too, it is far less frequent. As a comparison of expenses, annual expenses for ETFs range between 0.1 percent and 0.65 percent and are deducted from the dividends, while index mutual funds, for example, charge anywhere from 0.1 percent to more than 3 percent.

Turnover. Portfolio turnover is the frequency with which managers buy and sell assets. Portfolio turnover can be determined by calculating either the total number of new securities purchased or securities sold—whichever is less—over a particular period (12 months is standard) and dividing the total net asset value (NAV) of the fund.

The higher the turnover rate, the higher the transaction costs. Since transactional brokerage fees, for example, are not included in a fund's operating expense ratio, significant additional expenses (which reduce your return) could result if the turnover rate is high.

What ETFs can do for your portfolio

ETFs make the construction of a well-rounded portfolio so much simpler. The wide variability of available ETFs makes them suitable for many different strategies and, when properly constructed, give investors instant exposure to their target markets. Moreover, they further diversify your portfolio, and do so in a way that is highly liquid and relatively inexpensive. They also reduce your risk, which is especially important when the market is declining.
Here is a listing of the most popular ETFs:

Spiders (ticker symbol SPY)

SPDRS, or Standard & Poor's Depository Receipts, track the S&P 500 Index. Well diversified with relatively low risk, Spider is the best choice for new investors. Buying a share of a Spider is like buying a share of the Vanguard 500 Index Mutual Fund, with much added flexibility.

Diamonds (DIA)

If you like to invest in the well-known Dow Jones Industrial Average, Diamonds are for you. The Diamonds tracking the performance of the 30 largest companies in the United States represent the Diamond Trust Series. This ETF could expose your portfolio to large-cap blue-chip stocks.

Cubes (QQQQ)

Cubes corresponds to the 100 largest nonfinancial companies listed on the NASDAQ stock market. This ETF, which refers to PowerShares QQQQ, has been one of the most actively traded ETFs in the United States. Owning shares of Cubes brings you good exposure to the technology sector, which includes computer hardware and software, telecommunications, and biotechnology. However, it does not contain any financial companies.

MidCap 400 Spiders (MDY)

Standard & Poor's MidCap 400 Spiders, which track the S&P MidCap 400 Index, are a good addition to your investment portfolio for exposure to midsize companies in the U.S. security market.

iShares Russell 2000 (IWM)

This ETF tracks the Russell 2000 Index, which adds exposure to mid- and small-cap companies for your portfolio. The Russell 2000 Index represents U.S.-listed companies with market capitalization between $20 million and $300 million.

iShares MSCI EAFE (EFA)

This ETF is a popular way to add exposure to the top large-capitalization foreign markets. The iShares MSCI EAFE Index Fund tracks the MSCI EAFE Index, which includes all major economies (except that of the United States) and no emerging markets

Total Stock Market VIPERs (VTI)

A good proxy to including the U.S. economy in your portfolio is the Total Stock Market VIPERs. This ETF, sponsored by the Vanguard Group, tracks the Wilshire 5000 Broad Market Index, which is one of the broadest indexes for the U.S. equity market.

iShares SmallCap 600 (IJR)

This ETF, which is tracked by S&P SmallCap 600 Index, provides proper exposure to U.S. small-capitalization companies.

Now that we have discussed how to create a winning portfolio, it's time to learn how to manage that portfolio for maximum performance.

Part III

Monitoring Your Investment Portfolio with a Winning-Edge Investment System

Chapter 15:
Technical Analysis vs.
Fundamental Analysis

A key difference of the new-investment paradigm from the old one is taking a more active role in monitoring your portfolio; that is, regularly reviewing the securities or ETFs that make it up. At any given time, you should know which security has reached peak performance, which one's not performing as expected, and which one has more potential. Your goal in such monitoring is to determine which ETFs should be part of your portfolio and which should not, and then to rebalance your holdings accordingly to maximize performance.

There are two primary methods to monitor your portfolio: fundamental analysis and technical analysis. Fundamental analysis seeks to find an undervalued security to buy or an overvalued security to sell. Similarly, technical analysis looks for oversold conditions to buy and overbought conditions to sell.

Fundamental analysis

According to fundamental analysis, markets can misprice a security in the short run but then find and correct it to its "fair value" in the long run. In turn, an investor using fundamental analysis would look for such an opportunity to make a profit.

The main premise behind fundamental analysis is that, ultimately, a company's stock value is governed by the firm's profitability. As such, the primary tools of a fundamental-analyst investor is the company's financial statement and ratio analysis. The investor then uses different stock- and bond-value models to determine the underpriced or overpriced security. There are two major problems with this approach, however. First, the information is old and has already been considered or discounted by other investors and market participants. Second, as confirmed by behavioral finance findings, despite their use of such information for decision-making, investors actually tend to make decisions based on emotions and justify them via rationalization. This phenomenon is evident in the market when a certain stock is widely sold despite good news about the company. Or when investors buy a stock despite the company's negative earnings and poor financial health.

Fundamental analysis utilizes two methods to identify an undervalued or overvalued security: top-down and bottom-up. Top-down analysis begins with a general, macro view of a security and then narrows down to more specific information in a particular area. The analysis begins with consideration of the state of the economy, the business cycle, the fed's monetary policy, and the government's fiscal policy. The next step is to analyze the health of the industry that the firm belongs to, as well as the firm's industry life cycle, rate of growth, and level of maturity. Finally, the analyst performs a ratio analysis for the company, often using ratios to reveal a firm's state of liquidity and profitability.

A bottom-up fundamental analysis seeks and then explores companies who exhibit leadership and projection for growth and profit, regardless of macro factors such as the industry and economy.

Successful investors know, however, that using fundamental analysis alone does not help to identify a buying or selling opportunity.

Technical analysis

Using technical analysis doesn't necessarily reject the value of fundamental analysis, however. Technical analysis enables the new-paradigm investor to identify potential shifts in a security's price behavior, including the start of a new trend or the end of a long-lived trend. If a security has been advancing and making new highs, for example, the investor is poised to project its turning point—an overbought condition of the security—at which point, he can sell his positions, protect his profits, and create a much better return in the end.

The main tools used for technical analysis are a security's price chart and trading volume. The astute investor looks at different *chart patterns* and uses indicators called *technical indicators,* striving to exploit recurring patterns and historical price activity to generate high investment returns and trading profits.

If the information indicates that a company's liquidity, solvency, and profitability are positive, the investor might assume a higher demand for it, which would drive up the price. In fact, increased buying might even send the price to a level that seemingly includes or discounts new information, even when it does not. This level is called a *ceiling* or *resistance.* To get past this resistance level, market participants must buy more and push the price yet higher, which would require still more positive information.

On the contrary, if a security appears to be overvalued and would presumably not generate any meaningful profit, the investor would sell. Aggressive investors may even short-sell, which would cause the price to fall to what's called *floor or support level,* to adjust for proper valuation.

Bar charts

Several types of price charts can be used to depict price action and market behavior. The most popular type in investment management is the bar chart. This type is also more popular on the Internet and, therefore, easily accessed for free. Nevertheless, the Winning-Edge Investment System, which we'll discuss in future chapters, is equally equipped with other types of charts such as candlestick charts, and figure and point charts.

Investment bar charts typically depict price changes. As illustrated in Figure 15.1, each bar shows the opening price (denoted simply as *open*) and the closing price (or *close*) as well as the high and low prices (*high* and *low)* for a specified time period. Of course, there are slight variations among different bar charts: price action can be presented with a line that connects the close of each time period, for example, and various charts depict different time periods from minutes to months or longer. The Winning-Edge Investment System, for instance, uses a 30-minute chart, which features one bar for each 30-minute market price. It also uses a daily chart, which uses one bar for each day.

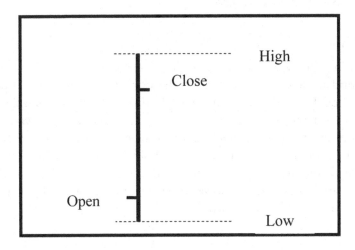

Figure 15.1. The four components of a bar from the standard bar chart used in investing: low and high indicate the low and high prices within a time period specified by the bar chart, and open and close indicate the opening and closing prices in relation to the same time period

Ned Gandevani, PhD

Technical indicators

A technical indicator uses mathematical calculations of past security prices to project future behavior. That's because technical analysts presuppose that any stock or market in general repeats its behavior.

Market behavior—in fact, any type of price move—can be indentified as either trending or trading (also called range bond). A trending security closes at sequentially higher prices (called an uptrend) or sequentially lower prices (a downtrend). However, a range bond or trading security has prices that are typically constrained between two price levels, the upper resistance and the lower support. When the price breaks out from a range, it may signify the beginning of an uptrend or downtrend.

In general, there are two types of technical indicators: momentum indicators and oscillators.

Momentum indicators

These indicators, which are generally used for longer time-frame investments, identify a trend and follow it. Examples of momentum indicators include moving averages, regression analysis, average true range, and ease of movement. In a long-term uptrend market, momentum indicators could help you manage your positions better or find the support level in order to buy a security. Let's review the two most common momentum indicators: trend lines and moving averages.

Trend lines

Trend lines show overall market direction, indicating an upward or downward move on a bar graph. (If the market is neither in an uptrend or downtrend, it's said to be sideways.) To draw an upward trend line, you connect the lows of the bars. As Figure 15.2 depicts, the upward trend line (also called a support trend line) is connected to the pivot lows. In an uptrend, investors expect the market to hold the trend line as a floor for its price action and gyrations. If the market penetrates and breaks down, however, they conclude the upward trend is broken or, at the very least, question the trend line's validity.

Figure 15.2. A support trend line connects the lows of bars to form a support and a floor for any possible downward move in the market

A downward trend line connects the bars' highs or pivot highs to create a resistance (see Figure 15.3). For this reason, a downward trend line is also called a resistance trend line.

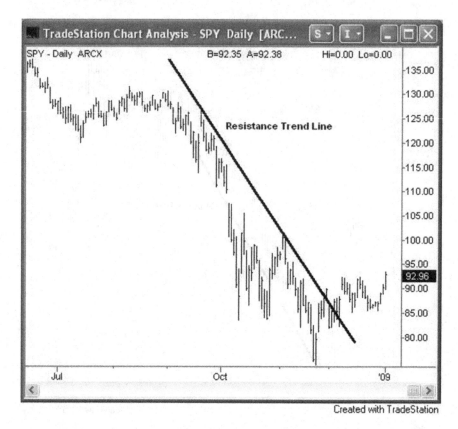

Figure 15.3. A resistance trend line connects the highs of bars and forms a resistance and a ceiling against a possible upward move in the market

To draw a trend line you need 2 points (i.e. on 2 different bars). However, to confirm a trending move, you need 3 or more such price points tracking movement within a timeframe—either for the long, intermediate, or short term, or for a combination of timeframes. Within a long-term trend, for example, you could track a few intermediate-term trends and many short-term trends. For any trend that you identified, you could assume a trending market would stay intact until the prevailing trend is violated.

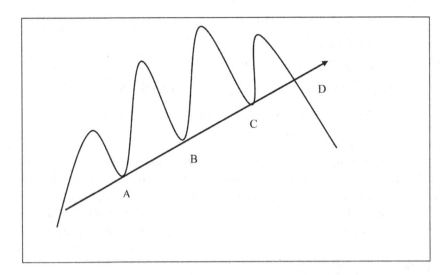

Figure 15.4. Price Points A, B, and C confirm an upward trend; however, at Price Point D, the trend is being violated

Consider Figure 15.4, which depicts an uptrend in a security. To establish a trend line, you'd need at least 2 price points, such as A and B, but to confirm an uptrend, you'd need Point C as well. When the security price falls, it requires the equivalent of Price Point D to indicate that the trend is no longer valid. At that point, you could exit your position by selling the security. Or, if you're an aggressive investor with high risk tolerance, you could either short-sell the security and buy it back later or cover your position at a lower price for profit.

Moving averages

Another popular momentum indicator is the moving average, which tends to "smooth" a data series to enable you to spot a trend more easily. These types of indicators are especially helpful in volatile markets.

A moving average (MA) is a calculation of the average (mean) price of a security or market index over a specified *number* of time periods. And while it is possible to create MAs from the open, high, and low data points on a bar graph, most MAs are created using the closing price. For example, a 3-day simple MA is calculated by adding the closing prices for the last 3 days and dividing the total by 3 as shown below:

> Close of Day 1 = $1,181.70
>
> Close of Day 2 = $1,189.20
>
> Close of Day 3 = $1,193.20
>
> $1,181.70 + $11,89.20 + $1,193.20 = $3,564.10
>
> $3,564.10/3 = $1,188.03 or, rounded off, $1,188.00.
>
> Daily MA = $1,188.00

The calculation is repeated for subsequent time periods. The resulting MAs of several consecutive time periods are then joined to form a smooth curving line, called the moving average line. So if we continuing with the example above, let's say the closing price of Day 4 is $1,192.00. To calculate the subsequent 3-day MA, then, you'd add $1,192.00 to the equation and subtract the closing price from Day 1—oldest day. The new 3-day MA would be calculated as follows:

($1,189.20 + $1,193.20 + $1,192.00)/3 = $1,191.46 or, rounded off, $1,191.50.

MA indicators and charting programs are commercially available in both brick-and-mortar stores and on the Internet.

There are different types of MAs that you could use to manage trading, such as simple, exponential, and weighted MAs. These indicators don't provide any advantage for short-term or swing trading, but are used mainly for exit and stop loss price levels. However, you may track 50- and 200-day MAs for your daily chart, since the market seems to pay particular attention to these two. Figure 15.5 illustrates the above mentioned three types of MAs.

As mentioned, most investment managers like to use 50- and 200-day MAs to help them manage their portfolios. Figure 15.6 illustrates a daily chart for the S&P 500 Index ETF, SPY. As the chart depicts, on December 27, 2007, after the market took out the slow 50-day MAs, the MAs acted as a resistance level until April 1, 2008. At that point when market moved higher, the 50-day MA behaved as a support level until it was broken again on June 6, 2008. The 200-day MA acted as a good resistance level on May 19, 2008.

As a new-paradigm investor, you can use such information to monitor your portfolio or place new position. For example, when the 50-day MA was a support, you could've bought into SPYDR (read as spider) and sold your positions on May 19, 2008, pocketing a nice profit for about 9 points. Or if you are an aggressive investor, you could have experienced the same sort of security on May 20, 2008, buying back to cover some of your short positions on June 5, 2008, for about 5 points profit, and still in a short position for more profits to come.

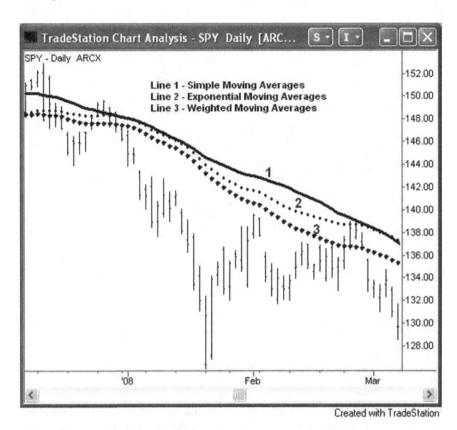

Figure 15.5. Three types of popular MAs. Line 1 is a 50-day simple MA. Lines 2 and 3 show exponential and weighted 50-day MAs respectively.

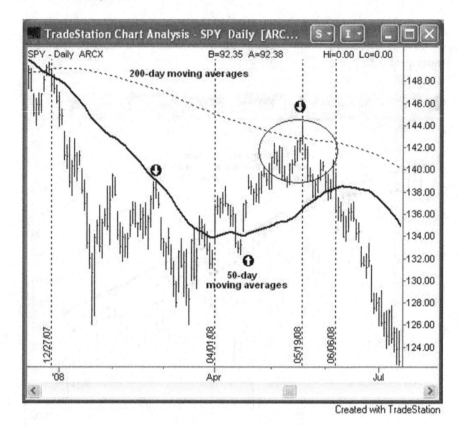

Figure 15.6. Two MAs shown on SPY daily chart.

Oscillators. The second type of technical indicator is an oscillator. Oscillators look to identify a high or low point, while considering that the market, as an aggregate of all securities, is influenced by economic cycles and, consequently, displays cyclical behavior. In addition, they recognize that each market cycle is divided into shorter cycles. Three of the most popular oscillators are the Moving Average Convergence and Divergence, the Relative Strength Index, and the Detrended Price Oscillator.

Depending on your timeframe, using a sound, time-tested oscillator could help you identify a probable high and low for the market or security you're monitoring. There are three major uses for oscillators, which are as follows:

1. To identify overbought and oversold conditions. If the oscillator crosses above the 70 percent line which is part of the oscillator readings on a bar chart, that indicates an overbought condition for the security and a possible top. Conversely, if the oscillator crosses under the 30 percent line, it depicts an oversold condition, meaning that its sales have been overextended and should soon see a turnaround in price. See the example in Figure 15.7, which uses one of the most popular oscillators called Relative Strength Index (RSI). In the chart, after the market crossed over the overbought boundary, the security, called QQQQ put a top in place and sold off. Conversely, after QQQQ reached the oversold line, or the 30 percent boundary, it turned around and took off.

Figure 15.7. The RSI confirming a high and a low for the security QQQQ

2. To identify divergence. Another important use of the oscillator is to identify a divergence between price action and the oscillator's readings. When the security price is making higher highs than the oscillator, it's called a *bearish divergence*. When a security price is making lower lows than the oscillator, it's called *bullish divergence*. Such diversions are important concepts that, as a new paradigm investor, you should take advantage of. Consider the chart in

Figure 15.8, which illustrates diversion between financial security XLF and another popular oscillator called the Detrended Price Oscillator (DPO).

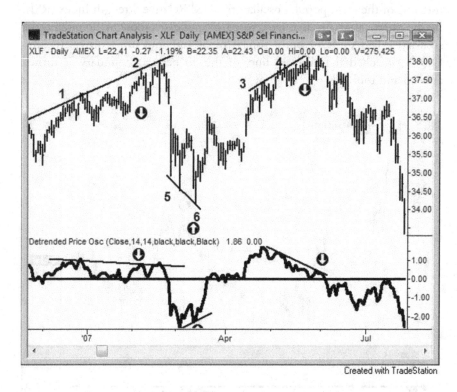

Figure 15.8. Divergence points between security XLF and the DPO

In Figure 15.8, the security, XLF, has made higher highs between Price Points 1 and 2, while the DPO has made lower highs—a bearish divergence. The same type of diversion occurred between Price Points 3 and 4. XLF sold off in both cases of bearish divergence.

When a bullish divergence occurred, however, the XLF took off due to the low prices. The oscillator was able to confirm a short-term low, which could be profitable for an investor. Suppose you were holding this security, and you observed the bearish divergence at Price Points 1 and 2, or 3 and 4. Wouldn't you sell your holdings? Of course you would. This is how a new-paradigm investor increases investment returns. Meanwhile, the old-paradigm investor who subscribes to the buy-and-hold strategy would have to suffer all of the losses.

3. To identify zero-line crosses. The third usage of oscillators is considering the zero line. Each oscillator inherently moves around a zero line that separates negative values from positive ones. When an oscillator crosses above the zero line, it could indicate an uptrend. Conversely, when the oscillator crosses to below zero, it could indicate a downtrend. Figure 15.9 depicts this concept for SPY, an ETF that represents the S&P 500 Index. The MACD Average line moves over the zero line, indicating a new uptrend.

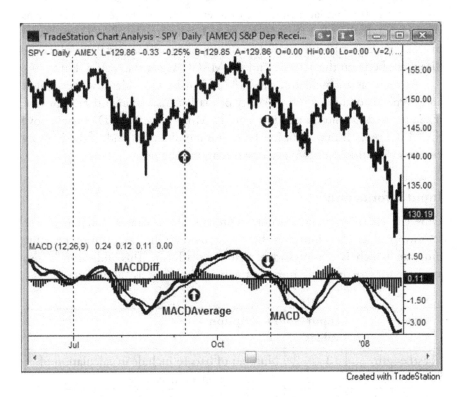

Figure 15.9. Monitoring movement around the zero line, using the oscillator MACD. The crossing of the MACD line over the zero line indicates an uptrend for the security.

Also keep in mind that you can use oscillators in a combination of ways, for example, to identify divergence and to confirm a low or high for a security. Now, let's go over the three most widely used oscillators in more detail.

Moving Average Convergence and Divergence (MACD)

The Moving Average Convergence and Divergence indicator is among the most popular oscillators, as it can be used both as an oscillator and a momentum indicator.

The MACD calculates two exponential MAs for the time period you specify: FastLength and SlowLength. FastLength measures an exponential MA with a short interval, while the SlowLength determines the same for a long period. The oscillator plots the difference between these two averages as the MACD. It also plots the MA for MACD, denoted by MACDAvg, based on the number of bars indicated in the input variables. Finally, it plots the difference between the MACD and the MACDAvg as the MACDDiff.

As such, as an oscillator, the MACD can be used identify overbought and oversold conditions for a security or market. As a momentum indicator, it can be used to follow a trend as would a MA—if the MACD crosses above the MACDAvg, it may indicate the beginning of an uptrend; if the MACD crosses below the MACDAvg, a downtrend may be near.

Input information

Different charting programs may represent input names differently. The following table, 15.1, indicates the setting used by the TradeStation charting program which is a professional trading platform. This indicator is also available for free on many Internet financial sites such as Yahoo Finance.

Name	Input values	Description
FastLength	12	Number of bars to include in calculation of the fast exponential average.
SlowLength	26	Number of bars to include in calculation of the slow exponential average.
MACDLength	9	Number of bars used to calculate the MACD exponential average.

Table 15.1. Input information for a MACD indicator

Figure 15.10 illustrates MACD on a daily chart for XLF, the financial ETF. The thick line depicts MACD while the thin line shows MACDAverage. The histogram graph represents the difference between fast and slow MAs.

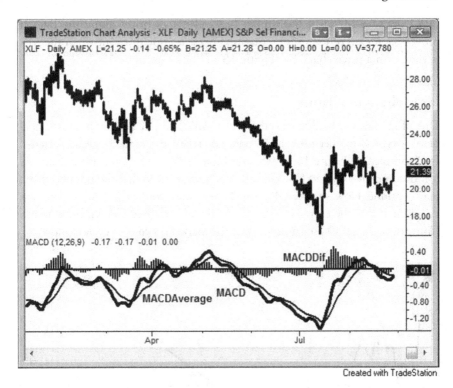

Figure 15.10. MACD indicator on the XLF daily chart

Relative Strength Index (RSI)

The Relative Strength Index calculates a value based on the cumulative strength and weakness of a price over a period of time., RSI accumulates the points gained on bars with higher closes and the points lost on bars with lower closes. These two sums are indexed and plotted on the chart as an oscillator with a value from 0 to 100. The direction of the RSI oscillator should confirm price movement. For example, a rising RSI would confirm rising prices.

RSI can also help identify divergences. For example, a new high in price without a new high in RSI may indicate a false price breakout. In other words as the security price is making higher highs that may not continue. RSI is also used to identify overbought and oversold conditions when the RSI value reaches extreme highs or lows. Figure 15.13 shows the use of an RSI as a technical indicator.

Detrended Price Oscillator (DPO)

As mentioned earlier, the Detrended Price Oscillator is similar to a MA, in that it filters out trends in prices in order to more easily identify cycles. The

DPO draws a MA as a horizontal line and places prices along the line. It provides a means of identifying underlying cycles not apparent when the MA is viewed in a price chart. See Figure 15.11 for an example.

More about oscillators

One of my favorite oscillators is the DPO, which I'd like go over in more detail here. A typical market price chart may not reveal the market's cyclic patterns. For example, see Figure 15.11 which exhibits SPY (read spider) price chart. As it moved up from point 1 to point 2, one may assume that the uptrend move may continue. However, the DPO oscillator did not confirm it. On the contrary, it indicated that the corresponding points 3 and 4 formed a down trend move. Conversely, the DPO oscillator revealed the market down turn cyclical move.

Figure 15.11. Divergence between the market price and the DPO, which may indicate the security price to discontinue its upward move.

A main focus of the new-paradigm investor is to determine short-term high and low price points. Identifying a short-term high enables us to take a short position or exit our long position. On the reverse side, knowing where the *probable* high or low is enables us to sell or buy the market for a profit. We could also use intermediate-term highs and lows to exit our positions.

If, for example, you hold a long position, and you identify an intermediate- or short-term high, it would make sense to sell your position for a profit. Or, you could move your trailing stop to lock your profit. A trailing stop is a stop-loss order, which you could adjust according to the favorable market move from your entry price. By using a trailing stop order, you can replace your original stop-loss order with a new one to protect your profit in case of an adverse market move. Accordingly, if the market continues upward, you could manage your position by moving your trailing stop up farther.

Repetitive patterns of price movement create market cycles, and many securities and markets tend to move in cyclical patterns. By identifying such patterns, the DPO indicator determines turning points in the market—that is, certain highs or lows that could arise due to recurrent external factors, such as seasons, elections, fluctuations in market participants' psychology and other underlying cycles not apparent from observing a price chart.

As shown in Figures 15.12 and 15.13, divergence between price levels and the oscillator readings can be used to identify the market's potential turning points.

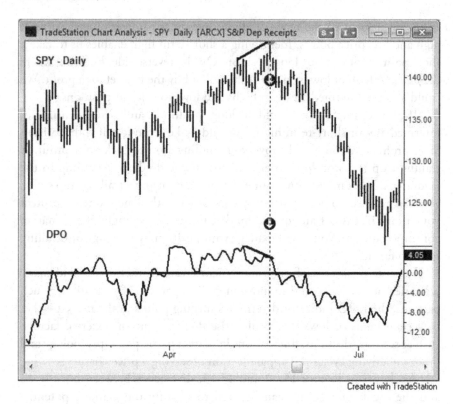

Figure 15.12. Divergence between the market price and the DPO, which can identify a potential reversal in the uptrend, generating a sell signal

Figure 15.13. Illustration of how a divergence between price and DPO can generate a potential buy signal

RSI and DPO combined-signals confirmation

I will go over this topic in more detail in the next chapter, but for now, just know that it's possible to use another oscillator—the Relative Strength Index (RSI)—in conjunction with the DPO to increase the probability of accuracy that the readings you get from the DPO for a signal confirmation or of a potential reversal in a trend line. Figure 15.14 exhibits how the RSI indicator correctly identifies the turning points in the market

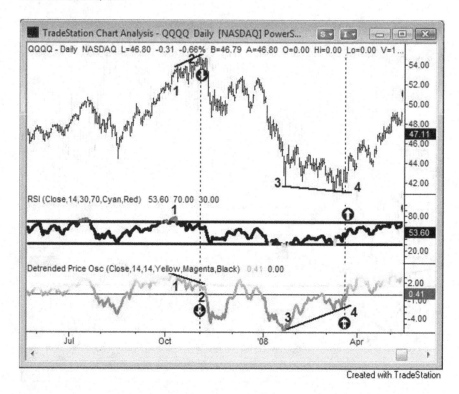

Figure 15.14. Example of how one can combine RSI and DPO indicators to confirm signals for better investment decisions

Market retracement levels

A popular concept in investment management is retracement levels. In a trending market, as the price moves up and attains new highs, it can reach a point in which the flow of buyers levels off, whereby it loses its uptrend momentum. Since the market can't find any more buyers, sellers come to short the market, at which point, the retracement theory proposes, the market could move down, traveling in a step-like fashion to levels such as 75 percent, 50 percent, and 25 percent. Conversely, in a downtrend, the market would rise in step-wise format from the lowest low to its highest price point.

Market retracement is only one tool that you can use to manage your investment holdings, however, and it may not work all of the time. Nevertheless, the majority of short-term trades require the use of this concept.

Fibonacci retracements

Leonardo Fibonacci, an Italian mathematician, was born in the 12th century. His study of the Great Pyramid of Giza and rabbits' breeding habits led to his discovery of the relationship of Arabic numbers. Soon after, he developed what became known as Fibonacci numbers, a sequence of numbers in which each number is the sum of the two previous numbers. Here is the Fibonacci sequence:

1, 1, 2, 3, 5, 8, 13, 21, 34, 55, 89, 144, 610, etc.

So, in creating such a sequence, for example, to get the next value after 13, you'd add 8 to 13 and arrive at 21. Likewise, to arrive at each successive number, you simply add together the two previous numbers.

In addition, if you take any two adjacent numbers and divide each by the sum of the two, the values converge to 38.20 percent and 61.8 percent (see Table 15.4).

1, 2	1÷3 =	33.3%	2÷3 =	66.7%
2, 3	2÷5 =	40 %	3÷5 =	60%
3, 5	3÷8 =	37.5%	5÷8 =	62.5%
5, 8	5÷13 =	38.5%	8÷13 =	61.5%
8, 13	8÷21 =	38.1%	13÷21 =	61.9%
13, 21	13÷34 =	38.2%	21÷34 =	61.8%

Table 15.2. The Fibonacci sequence has an interesting property. If one number is divided by the next one in the sequence, the result yields approximately 62 percent

What may be more interesting still is that any given Fibonacci number is approximately 1.618 times the preceding number and about 0.618 times the following number.

Many securities, after making sustained moves in either an upward or downward direction, eventually retrace back to levels that are consistent with the percentages gotten through such calculation of Fibonacci price retracement numbers; namely 23.6 percent, 38.2 percent, 50 percent, 61.8 percent, 76.4 percent, and 100 percent. So , to do a Fibonacci retracement (Fib retracement), just draw a trend line between the most recent peak and valley. Then subtract the peak value from the low value and divide it by 23.6 percent, 38.2 percent, 50 percent, 61.8 percent, 76.4 percent, and 100 percent. Values corresponding to the Fibonacci levels are potential market retracements, which you can use to predict future movement of the market and thereby manage your security more effectively. Since there is a high degree of subjectivity in choosing the peak and the low, you may end up with many potential retracement levels, but each would be valid until the market invalidated them.

Figure 15.15 depicts a daily chart for SPY. After making a low at 1,09.00 on October 24, 2004, the market moved up to 121.76 on January 3, 2005. The Fib retracement levels for this security would be calculated as follows:

121.76 (recent high value) – 109.00 (recent low value) = 12.76
38.2% level = 12.76 × 38.2% = 4.87 points
1,21.76 – 4.87 = 116.89 price level

50% level = 12.76 × 50% = 6.38 points
121.76 – 6.38 = 115.38 price level

61.8% level = 12.76 × 61.8% = 7.89 points
121.76 – 7.89 = 113.87 price level

According to the Fibonacci concept, one could guess that the market would pull back to 116.89 first, but given that the market were in a strong uptrend move, would not go down much further and would in fact resume its upward move after dropping to 116.89.

If the market reached the 50 percent area115.38—the uptrend may not be strong. And if it moved all the way down to 113.87, the uptrend would be suspect and the odds greater that the market could reach its previous low at 109.00.

But then how do you use Fib retracement to manage your trades? If you were holding a short position, you could scale out some of your position when you saw that the market was gravitating to areas around 1,16.89. Or you could just trail your stop to lock some of your profits. Then if the market kept moving down to areas around 115.38, you'd cover some more positions and move down your trailing stop to lock your profit and so on.

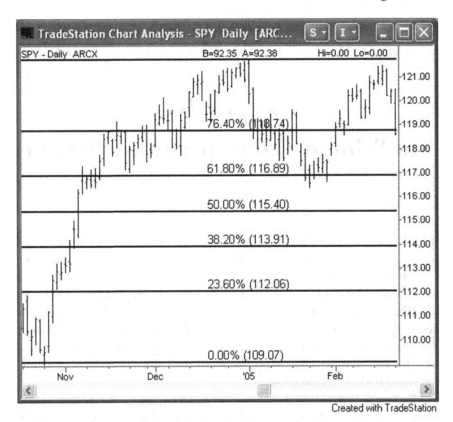

Figure 15.15. Fibonacci levels that one could use to manage positions

In the next chapter, we'll discuss how to use the Winning-Edge Investment System for optimum performance of your favorite security.

Chapter 16:
The Winning-Edge Investment System

In this section, we will discuss the details of the Winning-Edge Investment System for generating better investment performance. First, however, , let's study the characteristics of a sound investment system.

Jack D. Schwager, a financial author in his book *Market Wizards*, identifies the "common denominators" of top traders. One of those common denominators, he wrote, was that "Each trader had found a methodology that worked for him and remained true to that approach." It's significant, too, that the word Schwager most frequently used in his interviews regarding successful traders was *discipline*.

Success in investing and trading is based on two particular pillars: system (or methodology) and trader psychology. These two factors are so intertwined that they create a virtual circle: A better trading methodology will improve the investor's self-confidence. This improved psychological outlook will prompt the investor to adhere to the chosen methodology, which will then, consequently, boost the investor's performance and thus, again, his or her mindset.

For that reason, it's difficult to build a success in investing with only one of these pillars. A poor or nonexistent trading methodology can yield negative results, which can discourage an investor from consistently applying his method, which can result in lost opportunities and unfulfilled expectations, which in turn reduces the investor's self-confidence. It is therefore imperative that a serious investor consider both trading pillars as crucial to any investing activity.

What is an investment methodology or trading system?

An investment system is a collection of rules and methods that can help you identify entry and exit price points for a security or market—trading signals that tell you when to buy a security and when to sell it. (Or, if you are an aggressive investor, when to short-sell and when to cover your position.) In turn, the system should be executed by a serious, systematic investor.

There are two general types of trading systems: mechanical and nonmechanical. A mechanical system is a stand-alone trading system in which all of the money management is performed by a computer program. A mechanical system could be programmed to send generated signals directly to your brokerage account, for example. The main advantage of this system is that it works independently of emotions and human error. However, this advantage can also be drawback, since it's unable to account for real-time market conditions for better decisions.

A nonmechanical system is a set of rules by which you analyze price behavior. Of course, the more clear the rules, the better your performance. A great advantage of this type of system is its consideration for real-time market conditions and current events, but it has its drawbacks as well—namely, that human error factor.

The Winning-Edge Investment System is a nonmechanical trading system with objective rules. It aims to increase your investment performance by applying time-proven rules while also taking real-time market and security conditions into consideration. You may remember from our discussions in earlier chapters that a security price discounts and reflects all of the available information related to it. Therefore, a security chart price is one of the most effective pieces of real-time market information. The Winning-Edge Investment System uses two technical indicators: the RSI and the DPO, both of which provide sufficient information for sound investment decisions.

Benefits of investment systems

When you use an investment or trading system, you can reap benefits such as the following:

Less stress. Using a system to invest eliminates the stress of not knowing or second guessing at what price point to buy or sell. As part of your decision-making, you need to remember an array of variables, market conditions, and security data, all the while expending your best effort to avoid losing money; all together, this causes stress and emotional pressure. Relying on a set of rules that you have tested and gained confidence in, however, makes the process much easier. By simply following your investment system, you can operate comfortably to achieve your financial goals.

Optimum performance. Optimization is a process by which you refine the rules of an investment system for optimum results. The process is usually conducted via a computer program that contains sufficient historical data and security prices and allows you to see how a system would have performed differently in the past if you'd applied your "tweaked" rules. If you're not following an investment system, however, then you cannot optimize it and, thus, cannot optimize your returns.

Independence. Another great benefit of using a trading system is that you can always have someone else monitor your portfolio using the same system. This gives you a vast measure of independence and freedom.

Components of a trading system

Whether you developed a system on your own or purchased it, it should clearly state the rules and market settings for the following three system components: entry point, exit point, and protective stop. Let's go over each of these in more detail.

Entry point. Entry point is defined as the particular price point at which you should initiate a new holding, and it is determined by the rules and calculations of a particular investment method. In other words, your investment system tells you the precise moment at which you should enter the market. Entry point can be based on a market set-up, a signal, or a hybrid of the two.

1. Market set-up. In short, a market set-up is a price pattern or chart formation, which investors use to devise rules about when to enter the market. For example, "When the close of the second bar is higher than the close of the two previous bars on a 30-minute chart, buy at the open of the next bar." Or, "Buy the security at the breakout of an inverted head and shoulder before noon."

2. Signal. A technical indicator or specialized computer program gives mechanical signals in the form of arrows on your computer screen often accompanied by audible tones. A signal is generated by a series of calculations or conditions in the marketplace that may include technical as well as market-sentiment indicators. Market-sentiment indicators measure the market psychology which indicate whether market participants are bullish or bearish. A bullish sentiment depicts market could sustain further upward move. A bearish sentiment, on the other hand indicate that market could fall further.

For example using MA technical indictor, "If your 5-day MA crosses over our 10-day MA, you place a buy order."

3. Hybrid of market set-up and signal. As the name suggests, a hybrid uses both market set-up and signals to indicate entry point. For example, you might get a signal from your mechanical system and then confirm it with a market set-up tool, such as a chart formation.

Winning-Edge Investment System entry signals

As mentioned, the Winning-Edge Investment System uses two indicators— the RSI and the DPO—to confirm an entry signal and indicate an entry point. Similarly, every entry point should be initiated with two conditions— by DPO and RSI. A long signal happens when there is a bullish divergence between the DPO and security price bars and the RSI has crossed under oversold condition. Accordingly, a short signal occurs when there is a bearish divergence between the DPO and security price bars and the RSI has crossed above overbought condition. Details about these two types of signals follow.

Long signals. A long signal signifies a good price level at which to buy a security. It occurs when there is a bullish divergence between the DPO and security price bar at the same time the RSI has crossed below the 30 percent, or oversold, boundary. Figure 7.1 depicts a long-signal entry produced for a QQQQ ETF. The signal appears on a March 17, 2008, daily chart at $42.50, which then moves up to over $50.50, for a potential $8 profit, excluding commissions. At Price Point 4, the security made a lower low than Price Point 3, while the DPO made a higher low at the same price points; simultaneously, the RSI crossed under the oversold boundary at Price Point 3—the two conditions for a long signal.

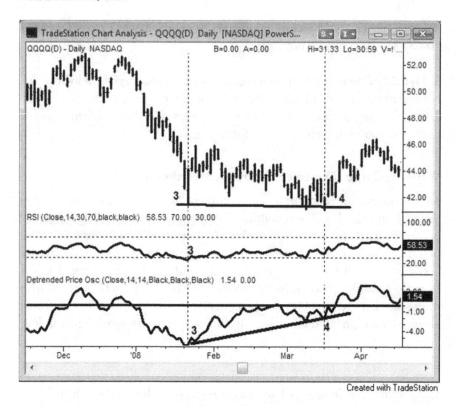

Figure 16.1. An entry signal generated by the Winning-Edge Investment System, which requires two simultaneous conditions: bullish divergence between the DPO and a price bar, and an oversold condition marked by RSI

Short signals. A short signal signifies a good point at which to sell or initiate a short-sell order. As is a long signal, a short signal occurs as a result of two simultaneous conditions: a bearish divergence between the DPO and security price bars, and a crossover of RSI above the overbought, or 70 percent, boundary. Consider Figure 16.2, which displays a short signal for a QQQQ ETF security. As the chart depicts, the QQQQ made a high at Point 2, which was higher than the price level at Point 1 while DPO made a lower high at price point 2—a bearish divergence. This satisfies the first condition. The RSI simultaneous crossing above the overbought 70 percent boundary provides the second condition. An investor could have used this signal to short the QQQQ from $54.50 and then cover it at least $43.50, a nice profit of $11, excluding commissions.

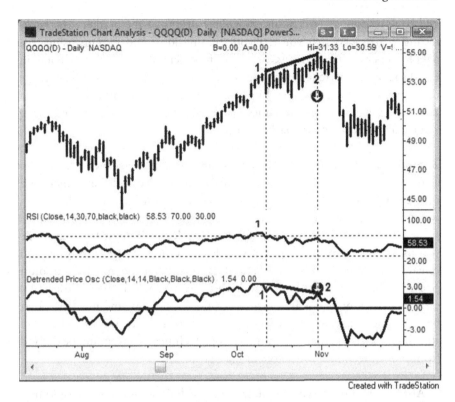

Figure 16.2. A short signal generated by the Winning-Edge Investment System, which requires two simultaneous conditions: bearish divergence between the DPO and price bar, and an overbought condition marked by RSI

Exit point. The exit point is a trading system's criteria to get out of the market. Before we even enter the market, we should either be aware of where our exit point will be or of what conditions will cause us to exit. We can accomplish such awareness in one of the following ways:

1. Target profit. One exit point can be earning your target profit. In other words, you plan to leave the market as soon as you make your intended profit.

To determine your target profit, you need to calculate your risk-to-reward ratio—a predetermined amount that expresses how much you're willing to risk versus how much you want to make. A ratio of 1:3, then, would imply that you're willing to risk no more than 1 unit in order to make at least 3 units.

Without a properly set ratio, the game of probabilities is hard to win, however. So don't forget to base your ratio on your psychological requirements and back-testing, as well as on your observations of the market. The back-testing is a process that you test your trading ideas and systems using past data for a period of a time. Assess the profit potential in a market, keeping in mind that a highly traded, active security will likely have a higher daily range than a thinly traded one. (And in a volatile market, you may see more of a daily range than during quiet times.) Ascertain the proper range by observing a particular security or via back-testing.

2. Stop loss. Remember that being wrong about an investment decision is as natural as being right; some of your trading choices will be winners and others will be losers. In fact, an inherent part of trading is loss. The key, then, is to make sure that you don't risk your total equity capital on one or even just a few trades. That's why you should set a stop-loss exit point for every trade you make. There are two types of stop-losses. One is a monetary stop, also called a price stop. In this type of stop-loss, you decide the monetary amount you're willing to risk for your trade. This dollar value can be as little as 10 cents per stock or as big as your total equity capital, an amount that is best based on the average volatility (price range) of the market. The second type of stop-loss, which I prefer, is a technical stop. Technical stops should be derived from proven technical indicators or market set-ups.

3. Abrupt change. As you monitor your portfolio's positions and holdings, watch for any exogenous market factors that could cause abrupt changes in a security's price or market conditions. For example, suppose you bought a security just before hearing unexpected but important news that will cause it to make an unusual move in the market. Depending on your position, you might need to take action to protect your investment. In other words, an abrupt change in the market may give rise to new or different stop-loss plans. If you detect that market conditions change (volatility for example) and your system's readings have altered, you should revise your positions immediately, regardless of any loss or profit.

Becoming the master of your portfolio performance in this way is one of the hallmarks of the successful new-paradigm investor. The old-paradigm investor, who primarily subscribes to the moribund buy-and-hold strategy, may not even care about an unexpected market condition. In fact, it always amazes me to know that many investors indeed take such a passive approach. They'll open a position and then leave it unattended until they get either stopped out or make a profit—whichever comes first. As mentioned, however, the new-paradigm investor considers adverse conditions and adjusts accordingly, based on a system's signals.

4. Timing. An experienced investor, after studying the character and internal dynamics of a market, can get a feel for how long a particular market can travel from a hypothetical Point A to Point B, thus predicting, on average, how many dollars per units of time it might gain. Armed with this kind of prediction, you can determine whether your position is making the appropriate amount and the trade is progressing at an appropriate speed. If it moves at a pace that is unacceptably inconsistent with your expectations, you may have to exit early. This concept of timing can be invaluable when used correctly. On numerous occasions, I have used such a technique to exit a trade before the market hit my monetary stop point, resulting in a winning or break-even trade, as opposed to a losing one.

Another timing method used frequently in financial markets is monitoring what are called fractal movements. Fractal movements are market movements resulting from the general (retail) public's market participation. Take the S&P financial market, for instance. Since the majority of retail traders in that market are undercapitalized, as the market moves 1 to 2 points, either for or against them, they typically jump out of their trades to cover with a small loss or gain. This constant flow of retail entry and exit activity has created a unique price fractal in the S&P market. An astute trader can easily capitalize on this idea, partaking in stress-free trades that are quite profitable.

The Winning-Edge Investment System's Exit Signals

The following exit signals generated by the Winning-Edge Investment System allow you to employ several possible strategies:

1. New signal. A bullish divergence is formed by the DPO and RSI, confirming a long signal, which means when you get a sell signal, you could exit long. Conversely, when the two indicators generate a bearish divergence, that would be a signal to exit or sell your position. Or if you sold short using a bearish divergence confirmation, you could cover your short position when indicators confirm a bullish divergence.

Consider Figure 16.3, which illustrates the DIA (pronounced diamond)ETF, holding 30 Dow Jones Industrial stocks. It portrays a short signal on October 11, 2007, at about $141. Then on March 17, 2008, you had a new bullish divergence to cover your short at about $119, a profit of $21 or about 16 percent.

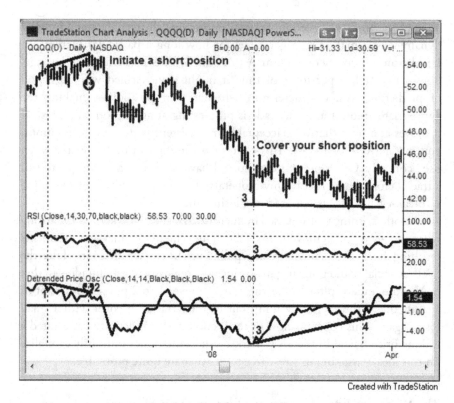

Figure 16.3. The Winning-Edge Investment System exit signal by creating a reverse signal to entry

2. One confirmation. Earlier, we discussed using double confirmations—DPO and RSI—as exit signals. However, you may often only need one such confirmation; for example, if the DPO forms a diversion signaling an exit. Figure 16.4 depicts a long signal on August 20, 2007. Having used the first confirmation in October 12, 2007as the exit signal, the bearish divergence between the price bars at Points 1a and 2a and the DPO Price Points 1a and 2a would have provided a quicker and more profitable exit. Similarly, price bar and DPO Points 3a and 4a offered an exit signal for the long signal generated on March 18, 2008

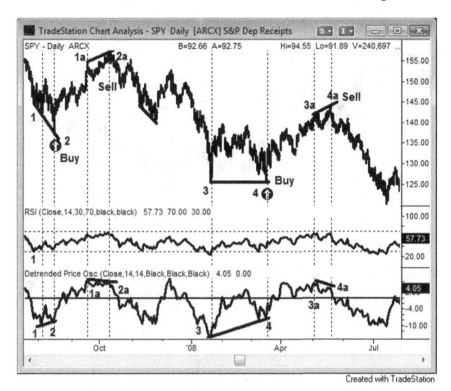

Figure 16.4. The Winning-Edge Investment System exit signal with only one confirmation

3. Moving averages. Another signal to exit a profitable position is called a moving averages crossover. In Figure 16.5, you'll see two 50- and 200-day MAs. You may exit some of your position when the security price crosses over the 50-day MAs, shown in doted line. (The illustrated circle shows the exit price.) Note: if you were using 200-day MAs, you'd still be in your short position, as prices decrease. Therefore, after using both types of MAs for some time, you could figure out which one worked better for you.

Figure 16.5. Illustration of how you could use 50- and 200-day MAs for exiting your investment positions

5. Retracement and fib numbers. In Chapter 6, we learned about Fibonacci price levels and how to use them as technical indicators to estimate a security's price movement. You can use the same method to retrace movement and exit at a better price. So, for example, if the market moved from a recent high say 150.00 in SPY (pronounced Spider) to a recent low 120.00, or vise versa. Then you could divide the total move 150-120 = 30 points by 3 and have 3 levels: 138.54 or 38.20 percent, 135.00 or 50 percent, and 131.46 or 61.80 percent. (While other retracement levels exist, they will not be covered here, as these three are the most commonly used by professional money managers and traders.)

Consider Figure 16.6, which identifies the high and low of a recent move, along with its various retracement levels. Note that security sold off after a short-sell signal generated by the system. Then it retraced back to 38.20 percent, 50 percent and 61.80 percent respectively, which corresponds to $125.59, $128.65, and $131.72. You could exit at one of those levels or just scale out your position as the price increased. For example, exit one-third at $125.59 and another one-third at $128.65and since the price did not hit the $131.72 retracement level, you could still be short and reap more profit as it dropped lower

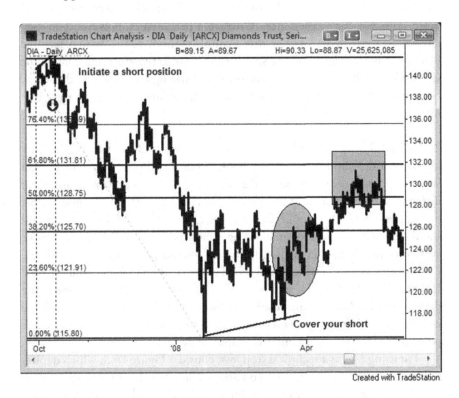

Figure 16.6. Using Fibonacci price levels as exit signals for profitable positions

The Winning-Edge Investment System's protective stops

Part of every winning system has losing trades. After all, any given system is based only on high probability at best, and it's natural to be wrong at least occasionally. In other words, it's okay to have losing trades, but how much of a loss is acceptable? It's crucial to answer that question in advance by identifying the price level or technical indicator that would provide ample warning that your security was not headed in the right direction.

For this reason, the Winning-Edge Investment System offers two types of protective stops. Let's go over each briefly.

1. Money stops. Assigning in advance how much of your capital you are willing to risk is placing a money stop. For example, you may decide based on your calculation and on the system's historical performance that you would not risk more than 3 percent of your capital. This means if you bought DIA (pronounced diamond) for $120, and it dropped 3 percent to $114.40, you'd sell it to exit your position and limit your loss. The smaller the percentage, the more stops you may experience. With large percentages, however, you may not be able to trade the security after a couple of times. One way to determine what price percentage might be suitable for a protective stop is to analyze the security's price fluctuations and volatility, and setting a stop at least that high. So, if a security's volatility is about 5 percent, having a stop at less than that may not be beneficial.

2. Technical stops. Another protective stop is a technical indicator. Any of the technical indicators in this book would qualify to help you protect your position against adverse market moves. Take MAs and trend lines, for instance. Suppose you're in long position, and the market price goes below the uptrend line; that could indicate you're not in the right position and should exit. Or, suppose you're holding a short position and the market price crossed over a MA; that may indicate you should exit your short position. Consider Figure 16.7, which exhibits a daily chart for SPY ETF, holding S&P 500 Index stocks. Suppose you bought the security at $126.50. As the figure depicts, you could exit your position at about Point B, when the uptrend line was violated. Alternatively, you could exit all of your positions when the price point dropped below your entry or purchase price.

For using MA as a technical stop loss, consider Figure 16.8, which depicts a daily chart for SPY. Suppose you short sold the security at 149.40. You could exit your short position at point A in the chart when price bar crosses over the 50-day MA. Or, trail your stop by moving down just above the MA. The latter action would lock your profit while gives you a chance to hold your short position. In case SPY sells off and price moves further down, you could exit at another point with probably better profit.

Figure 16.7. Using trend line as a protective stop and exit price.

Figure 16.8. Using MA as technical protective stop and exit price.

Chapter 17:
Types of Orders

As important as knowing where to buy and sell a security is knowing how to place your order so that you get what you ask for it. An order is an instruction to your broker either over the phone or online to buy or sell a security with certain conditions. When you open an equity brokerage account with a reputable, financially sound brokerage house, they may provide you with a list of order types that you can execute through their trading platform. It's important for you to familiarize yourself with this list, to know the order types they accept or reject. Otherwise, you may end up selling a security you meant to buy, miss an opportunity to execute a profitable trade, or place an improper stop-loss, causing you serious financial harm.

In the age of the Internet, knowing how to place your order becomes even more important to ensure any order you place is not rejected by the system.

There are several types of orders, each of which contain price and time restrictions for executing a transaction. Nevertheless, some orders may cost you more, depending on how easy or complicated it is for the brokerage house to handle.

In this chapter, we'll go over the essential basic orders accepted by almost any registered security brokerage firm. But first, let's discuss two possible positions you may have in a security. Having a good understanding about your position helps you to grasp trading orders better.

Long position

When you purchase a security, it's said that you are *long*. This means that if a security's price goes up, you could sell it at a higher price for a profit. Conversely, if its price goes down, you may have to sell it at a lower price for a loss. Therefore, "to exit your long position" simply means that you sell the security.

Short position (and short-selling)

If you think a security's price may fail to profit from selling, you may short-sell the security. This type of transaction is risky and requires serious consideration because if the price goes down, you make profit; however, if the price moves up, you lose money. Since the uptrend could be limitless, your associated risk of loss could also be without bounds. That's because you sell a security without originally owning it based on your credit worthiness and the margin required by your broker.

For example, let's say you short-sell ABC security at $50. It's then said that you are short ABC. To exit your short position, you will need to "cover your short." If you think that ABC security's price may drop from $50 to $45 you could place an order to cover your short at a $45 stop. Conversely, when ABC reaches $45, your broker would buy it to cover your short. At that point, you become "flat." Now let's take a look at the basic types of orders.

Market order

A market order is a simple, straightforward means to having your order executed or filled. By placing a market order, you are instructing your broker to buy or sell a security at the prevailing market price or at any price necessary to fill the order. This is a guaranteed way to do a stock transaction for relatively low cost, but could be very costly in a volatile market.

Each market order has two sides: the bid price and the ask price. The bid price is the price at which the market or security specialist offers to buy your security, while the ask price (also called an offer or sell price) is the price at which a security specialist or market is willing to sell it to you. Therefore when you place a market order, you get the highest bid to buy and a lower offer to sell.

Limit order

With a market order, you have to accept what price they offer you; with a limit order, you name your price and get what you want. A limit order, however, may cost a bit more commission and pose you to miss some good trading opportunities.

How? When you place a limit order to buy a security, your asking price will need to be above what the security is selling for, in order for you to get it. So say you want to go long with an ETF like SPY, which is traded at about $128.50. If you place an order to buy this security for $128.40, your order will not get filled and you will miss a potential upward move.

Stop orders (stop-loss and stop-limit orders)

You use a stop order to protect your profit or limit your loss. There are two types of stop orders: a stop-loss order and a stop-limit order.

A stop-loss order is essentially a request for a market order to be enacted when a particular security price hits a predetermined level that you set, known as the stop price. At that price point, your stop order "converts" into a market order and is filled accordingly.

For example, if you bought a security for $50 and wanted to protect yourself against a possible adverse move, you could place a stop-loss order, say, at $49.20. Once the security price hits $49.20, your market order is enacted and gets filled at that prevailing market price. With a stop-loss order, you may not know until after the transaction at exactly what price you sold your security, and if the market were volatile at that point, you might have gotten "a bad fill" with "slippage"—that is, had your order filled at a price lower than you'd expected.

Consider this example: You buy ABC security at a $45 stop; in other words, you ask your broker to buy the security when the price hits $45. At that $45 price point, your order "becomes" a market order, which means you may get $45or you may get or lower.

Thereafter, let's say the security price goes up to $50. You wish to "exit your long position" by selling it, so you place a $50 stop order with your broker to sell. As soon as the market hits $50, your stop order again becomes a market order and is filled accordingly.

The other type of stop order is known as stop-limit order, and should be used more to protect your profit than to stop potential loss. This type of order enacts or converts your order to a limit order rather than to a market order at the predetermined price point. And accordingly, the order is filled. With a stop-limit order, however, depending on market conditions and volatility, your order may or may not get filled. So think carefully when placing a stop-limit order.

Trailing stops

If you notice a market moving in a direction of your favor, you can use a trailing stop to lock in profit, by setting a stop at a price at which you want to sell in order to make a profit. Suppose you are long ABC security at $30, and the market price is now $40. You wish to protect your profit, but are not yet ready to sell. You could use a trailing stop, placing an order to sell ABC at $38. If the security price went down to that $38 point, your order would get filled, whereby you could lock in an $8 profit. However, if the price instead rose, your order would neither be triggered nor filled, and you'd still be long.

In that scenario, you could keep trailing up (or increasing) your stop until your price hit, and exit in a profitable position.

Day order or Good Till Canceled (GTC)

While a day order limits the fulfillment of your order to the same day, before or after which point, the order is void, a Good Till Canceled (GTC) order is virtually limitless; that is, the order is never void until it either gets filled or you cancel it.

All or none

Sometimes, often due to a stock's low trading volume, you may set the same price for all of the shares you've purchased or sold. Consequently, when you place an order, you may be required to set a condition as "all" or "none," which would instruct the broker either to fill all the shares for the same price or not to fill any. For example, you place an order to purchase 100 shares of SPY (ETF for S&P 500 index) at 95.20 as all or none. This means if your broker is unable to buy for you the shares for 95.00 each, could not fill your order. As you place such restrictions, you'd need to consider the trading volume and volatility of the stock.

In the next chapter, we'll discuss how the Winning-Edge Investment System works to monitor your portfolio. Using the proposed system you could increase your performance while minimizing your risk.

Chapter 18:
Working the Winning-Edge
Investment System

As explained earlier, there are two main stages to a new-paradigm investor's successful investing. The first stage is to construct a portfolio based on your RTI and overall investment strategy. Second, you should monitor and rebalance your portfolio according to the Winning-Edge Investment System.

Let's revisit the steps you should take to construct your portfolio for that first stage:

- **Indentify your investment goals.** Make sure those goals are SMART (Specific, Measurable, Attainable, Realistic, and tied to a Timetable), and remember the triple-A method to achieving them: Attitude, Attribute, and Action.

- **Identify your RTI.** Take the test in Chapter 4 to get your RTI score, which shows your risk tolerance and relates directly to your portfolio standard deviation. Use your RTI as a guide for adjusting your financial goals.

- **Allocate your assets.** Use your RTI or portfolio standard deviation to calculate the distribution of your investments among major asset types such as equity, bonds, and cash.

- **Select your assets.** Choose the proper Exchange Traded Funds (ETF) for your portfolio, paying attention to important measurements such as beta, alpha, and Sharpe ratios. The Sharpe Ratio which was derived by Prof. William Sharpe, is a measure of the risk-adjusted return of an ETF.

- **Monitor your portfolio.** Monitor the performance of your new portfolio using the Winning-Edge Investment System, adjusting it, as necessary, according to factors such as your age, financial needs, health, and future goals.

Now, let's look at a few extended examples that illustrate how you could put together all the parts discussed so far to help you successfully invest in these new times.

Example 1

Suppose you have $100,000 to invest. Your RTI is 10 percent, and your time horizon for this particular investment is about 10 years. Moreover, you do not rely on this money for your daily expenses and do not need to withdraw any part of it or its earnings for another 10 years. Using these numbers, let's start from the beginning and construct a winning portfolio, which we can later monitor for maximum performance.

With your RTI of 10 percent, you're considered a moderately aggressive investor, which translates to a portfolio standard deviation of 10 percent. You could use Table 9.6 to find the corresponding portfolio standard deviation for your RTI. To refresh your mind, I've placed Table 9.6 from chapter 9 below again.

Portfolio model	Risk Tolerance Index score	Risk Tolerance Index (RTI)	Asset or portfolio volatility (σ)
Conservative	18 or lower	Very low	5%
Moderately conservative	19–36	Low	7%
Moderate	37–54	Medium	9%
Moderately aggressive	55–72	High	11%
Aggressive	73 or higher	Very high	13%

Table 9.6. Risk-tolerance classifications based on total RTI test score

Let's consider two main asset classes since you don't plan to withdraw any funds for at least another 10 years. Using the formula 12.2 in Chapter 12, which is shown below

$$E(r) = W_1{}^* E(r_1) + W_2{}^* E(r_2) \qquad\qquad \text{(Formula 12.2)}$$

we can calculate the percentage of funds to invest in equities and bonds. Again for your convenience, I've pasted Table 12.3 below with shaded row.

Stocks, percent of allocation	Bonds, percent of allocation	Portfolio return	Portfolio standard deviation	Return-per-unit risk	Reward-to-variability ratio
0	100	5.8	8.7	0.67	0.32
10	90	6.44	8.09	0.80	0.43
20	80	7.08	8.08	0.88	0.51
30	70	7.72	8.66	0.89	0.55
40	60	8.36	9.72	0.86	0.55
50	50	9	11.13	0.81	0.54
60	40	9.64	12.78	0.75	0.52
70	30	10.28	14.59	0.70	0.50
80	20	10.92	16.49	0.66	0.48
90	10	11.56	18.47	0.63	0.46
100	0	12.2	20.50	0.60	0.45

Table 12.3. The expected performance, standard deviation, and reward-to-variability ratio for a portfolio with various asset allocations of two risky assets: stocks and bonds

Or for a quick, easy solution, use Table 12.3 in Chapter 12 to identify the corresponding bond and equity asset allocation for a 10 percent standard deviation. Following the information in that table, you'd invest 40 percent in bonds and 60 percent in equity. This asset allocation yields an expected portfolio return of about 8.5 percent.

So this is what we have for your portfolio so far:
Portfolio standard deviation = 10 percent
Portfolio expected return = 8.5 percent
Bond allocation = 40 percent
Equity allocation = 60 percent

For bond allocation, we could use an ETF such as the Vanguard intermediate-term bond. For the equity, we could use either SPY ETF or QQQQ ETF, which represents the NASDAQ 100 Stocks Index.

Now let's see what your performance could have been using the Winning-Edge Investment System from January 2007 up to now. Since your investment horizon is 10 years, we could use longer-timeframe charts to monitor both the bonds and equity portions of the portfolio.

The bond portion:

For the bond portion, as mentioned, we'll use the Vanguard intermediate-term bond ETF which trades in the Amex exchange under the ticker symbol BIV. This ETF provides high income potential to balance the risk in the remainder of your portfolio, which contains 60 percent of your investment capital. And with a low expense ratio of 0.11 percent, this security seems to be a good fit for our portfolio. Further, Vanguard has described its credit rating as similar to that of U.S. government treasury and agency bonds.

Let's say you invested on June 1, 2007, and that we'll analyze your portfolio's performance for just one year, ending May 30, 2008, excluding commission, which should be no more than about $120.

Suppose on June 1, we purchased the ETF bond BIV at about $74 per share. Since we're allocating 40 percent to this asset, we'd purchase $40,000 (40 percent × your total investment capital of $100,000), which would be 540 shares with a $40 commission. Or even better, we could have waited until the system generated a buy signal on July 9, 2007, then bought for about $73.10 per share (see Figure 18.1). Then on March 24, 2008, the system issued a sell signal to exit our long position at about $80, as it made an intraday high of $81.49. We could have either remained flat until May 30, 2008, or taken an aggressive approach and short the BIV at the same price as we exited our long ($80). In other words, if we'd been long 540 shares, we could have sold up to 1,080 shares, which would have exited our long and initiated a new short position at $80. Then on May 30, 2008, we could have covered our short position by buying the security for about $77 per share, resulting in the following performance for the bond portion of the portfolio:

Moderate approach

Purchased on June 1, 2007: 540 shares at $74 per share = $39,960
Sold on March 24, 2008: 540 shares at $80 per share = $43,200
Total holding return = (43,200 − 39,960)/(39,960) = **8.11 percent**

Aggressive approach

Purchased on June 1, 2007: 540 shares at $74 per share = $39,960
Sold on March 24, 2008: 540 shares at $80 per share = $43,200

Note that many brokers require you to open a margin account, or trade stocks with cash to sell a security short. Conversely, you need to keep between 30 to 50 percent of the total market value of the security for maintenance. In the hypothetical performance presented below, I use the most conservative short-sell by requiring 100 percent of the security price for maintenance, which means you'd be fine even if the security price dropped to zero. In other words, for this illustration's purpose, I assume that all the securities are purchased on cash and not margin.

Therefore, on a very conservative short-sell approach, we could have sold only 50 percent of our total bond equity, which would maintain 100 percent of our new short position. Conversely, we'd have sold short only 270 shares at $80 each.

Then, covering our short position on March 30, 2008, at $77 per share would have resulted in a profit of 270 × ($80 − $77) = $810, or $43,200 + $810 = $44,010

Total holding return = ($44,010 − 39,960)/(39,960) = **10.14 percent**

Ned Gandevani, PhD

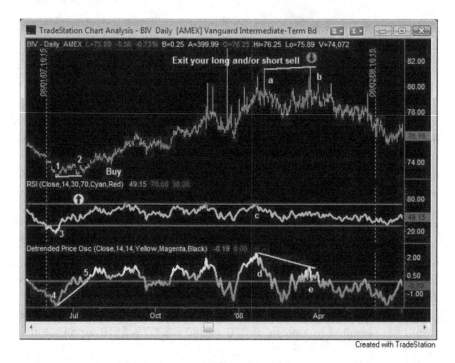

Figure 18.1. Entry and exit prices for the bond portion of the Example 1 portfolio in this chapter

The equity portion:

For the equity portion of the portfolio, we could use QQQQ ETF, which represents NASDAQ 100 Stocks Index. Since 60 percent of the total capital is allocated to the equity, we could have purchased the security on June 1, 2008 for about $47.50 per share. That would have given us 12,631 shares for $599,972.50. Then on November 1, 2007, we could have exited our long position as the system issued a sell signal at about $54 per share. We could have taken an aggressive approach and shorted the market at the same time. For a moderate approach, we'd have been flat and then bought the security on March 19, 2008, at about $43 per share. Finally, we could have sold the stock on May 30, 2008 for about $50 per share. So for the equity portion, depending how aggressive we wanted to be, we could have shorted the market on November 1, 2007 and covered our short on March 19, 2008 buying at twice the size of our short holding.

You should, as stated above, sell a security short when you have a margin account or use your cash account to maintain between 30 to 50 percent of

162

the total security market value. Therefore, to sell short the bond ETF BIV, we should keep 50 percent of the BIV market value in the account in cash. For this example, as I present the hypothetical performance below, I use the most conservative short-sell by designating 100 percent of the security price as a maintenance requirement. That means even if the price of the security dropped to zero, we would not have been called upon for a maintenance or margin requirement. In other words, for the illustration's purpose, I assume that all securities are purchased on cash and not margin.

Here are calculations for the equity's performance;

Moderate approach

Purchased 1,263 shares at $47.50 on June 1, 2008, for $59,992.50
Sold long position on November 1, 2007, at $54 per share for $68,202 (1,263 × $54)
Purchased 1,586 shares ($68,202/$43 = 1,586) on March 19, 2008
Sold the QQQQ on May 30, 2008, to exit our long position at $50 per share for $79,300 (1,586 × $50 = $79,300)
Total holding period return for
QQQQ = ($79,300 − $59,992.50)/$59,992.50 = **32.18 percent**

Aggressive approach

Purchased 1,263 shares at $47.50 on June 1, 2008, for $59,992.50
Sold our long position on November 1, 2007 at $54 per share for $68,202 (1,263 × 54)
Sold QQQQ on November 1, 2007, at 1,263 shares at $54 to exit our long position for $68,202. Alternatively, we could have sold short 631 shares at $54 to open a new short position and minimize any possibility for margin or maintenance call.
Purchased 631 shares at $43 each to cover our short position on March 19, 2008, resulting in a profit of 631 × ($54 − $43) = $6,941
At the same time, we'd have purchased $6,941 + $68,202 = $75,143 worth of shares at $43, which would have resulted in owning more than 1,747 shares.
Finally, on May 30, 2008, we could have sold all our shares at $50 per share for $87,350.
Total holding period return for
QQQQ = ($87,350 − $59,992.50)/$59,992.50 = **45.60 percent**

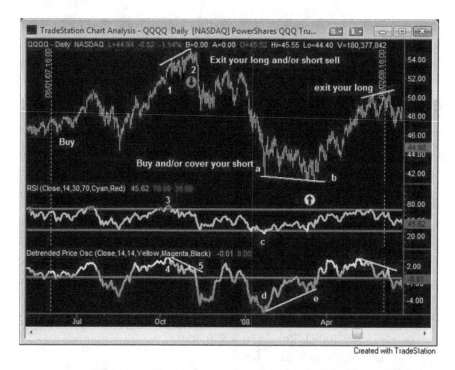

Figure 18.2. Workings of the Winning-Edge Investment System for the equity portion of the Example 1 portfolio in this chapter

Depending on the approach, your $100,000 from June 1, 2007, would have yielded the following results by May 30, 2008:

Moderate approach

$43,200 (40 percent bond portion) + $79,300 (60 percent equity portion) = $122,500 or 22.5 percent total holding period for one year

Aggressive approach

$44,010 (40 percent bond portion) + $87,350 (60 percent equity portion) = $131,360 or 31.60 percent total holding period for one year

Buy-and-hold approach

The bond portion:

Purchased on June 1, 2007: 540 shares at $74 per share = $39,960

Sold on May 30, 2008, to exit long position: 540 shares at $76.90 = $41,526

Total holding-period return = ($41,526 − $39,960)/$39,960 = **3.92 percent**

The equity portion:

Purchased 1,263 shares at $47.50, each on June 1, 2008, for $59,992.50

Sold 1,263 shares at $50 each on March 30, 2008, to close long position for $63,150

Total holding period return for the portfolio's equity portion =($63,150 − $59,992.50)/$59,992.50 = **5.26 percent**

Total holding period return for the portfolio:($63,150 + $41,526) − ($100,000)/($100,000) = **4.68 percent**

Using the new-paradigm-investment approach and, in particular, the Winning-Edge Investment System, you would have yielded a whopping return of 22.5 percent with a moderate approach or 31.60 percent with an aggressive approach. Table 18.1 summarizes the performance of the hypothetical portfolio that started with $100,000.

Hypothetical Performance for $100,000 Portfolio Using the Winning-Edge Investment System from June 1, 2007, to May 30, 2008				
Strategy		**Bond return**	**Equity return**	**Portfolio return**
Buy-and-hold strategy		3.92%	5.26%	4.68%
Winning-Edge Investment System	ModerateApproach	8.11%	32.18%	22.50%
	AggressiveApproach	10.14%	45.60%	31.60%

Table 18.1. Comparison of yields for a $100,000 investment using the buy-and-hold strategy versus using the Winning-Edge Investment System

Example 2

Now let's see how we could use the Winning-Edge Investment System with individual stocks. Many of you may have or be considering the purchase of some shares of a popular stock. The Winning-Edge Investment System enables you to maximize your performance by identifying the proper purchase price for various shares and using its information to make better decisions about whether to sell or keep particular stocks.

Let's look at Goldman Sachs (symbol GS) stock and see how you could have saved yourself from financial hardship by selling your position before its recent major correction. As Figure 18.3 depicts, the daily bar chart for the stock using the Winning-Edge Investment System would have provided a sell signal on June 8, 2007, when the stock price was at about $230. The DPO was in bearish divergence with the stock price bars. Further, the RSI indicator had reached the overbought boundary. As the system generated a sell signal, the stock price dropped to make an intraday low of $140.27 on March 21, 2008—a 43 percent price correction! If you are an aggressive investor, you could have even sold short the stock on June 8, 2007, and pocketed the profit when you covered your short positions on March 21, 2008, for just less than $90 of profit per share. This is a huge gain that only the new-investment paradigm would enable you to make.

Figure 18.3. The Winning-Edge Investment System sends indicators that would protect a portfolio from the recent Goldman Sachs stock drops.

Example 3

Suppose you hold the Vanguard Asset Allocation Fund (symbol VAAPX), a popular mutual fund, in your retirement plan. With the recent market volatility and negative performance, however, you've become worried about it. You are not sure whether to keep it or sell it. The Winning-Edge Investment System can help you determine the optimal price at which to sell your long positions.

By glancing at Figure 18.4, you can observe how powerfully the system was able to generate a sell signal on June 15, 2007, when the fund made an intraday high of $31.12. After the sell confirmation, it dropped to make an intraday low of $24.78 on July 17, 2008—about a 20 percent price correction. By using the system, you would have been able to save yourself from a great deal of heartache and misfortune. (Also note that as the mutual fund was making a higher high at Numbers 1 and 2, the DPO was making a lower high at Numbers 4 and 5—a bearish divergence that was confirmed by the RSI reaching an overbought condition and hitting the upper boundary at Number 3.

167

Figure 18.4. Weekly chart for the Vanguard Asset Allocation Fund. The Winning-Edge Investment System was able to confirm a sell signal to save you a bundle of hard-earned money.

So far, we've covered how to construct a winning investment portfolio and explored the components of the Winning-Edge Investment System to help you optimize your investment returns. However, knowing how to invest is only one part of being a successful investor. The other vital part is being able to *apply* what you know. Many investors know theoretically how to construct a good portfolio as well as how to monitor and rebalance it. However, a large gap often exists between their knowledge and performance; many fail to implement their knowledge effectively in real life, particularly under stressful conditions, resulting in relatively poor returns. The main cause of such a gap? Psychology. That's why in the next section, we'll learn about investment psychology, in particular, including psychological pitfalls and decision traps that can hinder your investment performance.

Part IV

Investment Psychology

Chapter 19:
Investment Decision Traps—
Heuristic-Driven Biases

Many investors, despite their in-depth knowledge of trading, are unable to generate positive returns consistently. That's because their past trading experiences inevitably color their perspectives, affecting the numerous detailed decisions they must make regarding future trading. Consequently, regardless of how proven their strategies may be, they fall short in following signals or recommendations correctly, which, in turn, drags down their performance.

At the root of this phenomenon is trading psychology and its influence on investment behavior. While I won't go too deeply into the larger topic of trading psychology here, one important aspect of it that you should understand— namely, because of its relationship to new-paradigm investing—is how to identify and thereby avoid the most common errors made by investors.

Here's an example. Imagine your system provided a buy signal to go long with the S&P. Since you're determined to follow your system, you take the signal and place the long trade with your broker. It turns out to be a losing trade. "Okay, that's fine," you say, trying to center yourself. Later, the system gives you another signal for a long trade. But now you're hesitant and need more time to justify the logic of making such a move. Ultimately, you decide not to take the signal, but it turns out to be a great trade. Sound familiar? If so, the key question to ask yourself is why you failed to take the second signal if you are determined to follow your trading system.

According to research and theories regarding decision-making (sometimes called behavioral decision theory) there are two fundamental reasons we succumb to such decision traps: heuristic-driven biases and frame dependence.

In general, heuristic-driven biases refers to errors encountered when making decisions. In decision-making, our minds tend to reference sets of guidelines or rules of thumb that it has constructed based on our past experiences, cultural influences, social values, biases, and other information. The other type of decision trap, frame dependence, generally refers to the way we make decisions based on what we see at that moment, (i.e., our perspective). In this chapter, I will delve into the heuristic-driven biases, while the next chapter will focus on frame dependence.

Heuristic-driven biases

The word *heuristic* comes from the Greek word for *discover*. In psychology, heuristics refers to the mental process by which a person, through trial and error, finds out something and, in turn, forms rules of thumb to guide their decision-making (2). Such a mental procedure, they say, is our brain's way of designing a shortcut, so that we can reach a decision with less time and effort. On the flip side, however, heuristics can inherently lead to errors in judgment and are the primary cause of decision traps (3).

Let's consider an example. Suppose the performance of a mechanical system is as follows:

Number of trades: 25   Number of winning trades: 15

When this system generates a buy signal, which of the following scenarios will most likely occur?

a. A winning trade
b. A winning trade, since there is a double-bottom chart formation above the 15-period MA.

When I posed this question to some clients, the majority of them chose *b* as the more probable outcome. Let's look closer. Given the above information, we know that the probability of scenario a is about 60 percent. In scenario b, several factors influence the outcome of the trade. In other words, rationally, the probability of a single event occurrence (scenario a) is greater than the probability of a co-occurrence of two or three events (scenario b). So according to decision science researchers, choosing *b* would be the result of a phenomenon called a conjunction fallacy (4).

Before we go further into decision traps, let me make a clear distinction between decision errors and decision traps. Decision errors occur when the operator of a system does not have all the information on which to base decisions. For example, when a trader isn't sure when to take a trade or when the rules of a trade are not distinctively defined. Decision traps, on the other hand, result when a trader faces psychological or emotional barriers in making trade-related decisions and are subsequently trapped by the resulting lack of discipline, unable to follow the original trading strategy.

Expounding on this idea of being psychologically trapped, Jim Reason, University of Manchester, asserts that any operator who is blamed for a system error often becomes the victim of a series of problems or errors. He coined the term "latent pathogens," to refer to problems such as poor design, poor training, and poor procedures that may go undetected until the operator falls into emotional and psychological decision traps (5).

Here are some general ways to avoid the heuristic-driven decision trap:

- Use a trading system that is compatible with your Trading Personality Profile (TPP). Your TPP encapsulates your personal characteristics, including your reactions under stress and uncertainty. (For more information about TPP, see the author's book *How to Become a Successful Trader—The Trading Personality Profile: Your Key to Maximizing Your Profit with Any System* (6)).

- Develop more confidence in your system by studying it hard and validating its viability on your own. Past performance is a good way to measure your system's merits, but is not enough to convince you to use it; you need to prove to yourself that your system is valid by applying it in real time with paper trading or using a small-capital allocation for testing purposes.

- Avoid information (including that given in news media coverage) that was not included in developing your system. Such information, though it may be helpful once or twice, will not benefit your overall trading program.

1. The "availability" trap

We all make decisions based on the information available to us, whether that information is accurate or not. Let me give you an example. A trader whom I'll call Dave had a difficult time following his system. After I conducted preliminary studies of his system, I discovered he was keen on using what's called a "squawk box" in his trading. When he heard that the noise level in the S&P trading pit was increasing, he got nervous and froze. In some cases, when he heard the pit reporter announcing a big order being placed to sell the market, he would not take the long signal.

In my interview with him, I asked, "In designing your trading system, did you ever consider the decibel level of the squawk box as a factor in your trading performance?" He replied with a definitive no.

Dave had fallen into the availability trap, basing his trading decisions on available information instead of on his own system's recommendations, which had been back-tested and validated for accuracy. Other sources of this trap could be a fax service from a "market guru" or a trading-information-based Web site. Even something as benign as a "floor broker" questioning an order you placed can wreak havoc on your ability to follow your own trading decisions. The availability heuristic is a common decision trap. It is an available shortcut to making decisions under uncertain and sometimes stressful situations.

As an investor, you can become ensnared in the availability trap for two primary reasons. The first reason is that you may not have full confidence in your trading system.

If your system's performance does not meet your expectations—that is, you have a few losing trades in a row—you may lose confidence in the system's viability and look for any outside information you can find that may help you increase your portfolio's performance.

The second reason you may fall into the availability trap is that your system is not compatible with your Trading Personality Profile (TPP). Remember, your TPP encapsulates your personal characteristics, including your reactions under stress and uncertainty. So, for instance, if your profile is not suitable for trading with a mechanical system, you may doubt the merit of such a system's recommendation and instead take any outside information that's available.

2. The "representativeness" trap

When people make decisions based on stereotypes, they fall into a representativeness trap. According to psychologists Kahneman and Tversky, a representativeness heuristic occurs when a judgment is rendered about one event based on the degree to which it resembles another event (7).

Investors who rely heavily on the historical precedence of certain market events, for example, are using such a heuristic, providing past events as support for their analyses of present market conditions, rather than seeing the current market in light of overall fundamental changes. And today's economic backdrop is much different from that of a few years ago.

Case in point: before coming to me for help, Jim was very frustrated with his protective stops in the S&P market. He could not figure out why almost every protective stop he placed was stopped out. He even wondered whether his broker had a grind with him. When I asked him how he selected the "right" protective stop, he said he looked at the past 10 trades, identified the highest stop, and placed his stop a few ticks above that. In other words, he was using a sample of his trades, assuming it was a fair representation of his system. He fell into the representativeness trap, creating a stereotype from a sampling that didn't necessarily resemble his system's true trades.

A good number of analysts lately have compared contemporary market events and conditions to those of the 1930s. They state that the Fed's recent rate cuts have set the foundation for a rate-hike agenda for the next 12 months due to the possible increase in inflation. In addition, with recent problems ignited by the technology sector bubble and the housing and credit bubbles, which has created a credit crunch, it's easy to look for historical precedence in order to offer new solutions. Failing to consider current fundamental shifts in the global economy, many are tempted compare raw data without looking at the new macroeconomic trends. This type of thinking (actually, lack of thinking) sets up the very dangerous snare that is the representativeness trap.

Joe, an active equity trader, noticed that any time the NASDAQ Index moved up, the broader S&P market also increased. So on a few occasions when his system provided a long signal and he noticed the NASDAQ simultaneously moving up, he acted on his system's recommendations and had some nice gains. Eventually, he got to where he would not act on a signal until he got "confirmation" from the NASDAQ. That is, until he hit a dry patch. For a week or two, he sat stagnant because the NASDAQ and the S&P had been moving in opposite directions. Meanwhile, Joe wondered why he no longer was following his system's great signals. When we discussed his situation, I learned that he'd never done an intermarket analysis between the S&P and the NASDAQ but that, nevertheless, he'd started using intermarket analysis as a confirmation for his system. It became clear to me then that he had fallen into the representativeness trap.

The following are some of the different forms and variations of the representativeness trap and how they may impact us.

a. The "gambling fallacy" trap

Allen had a string of successful trades that, naturally, excited him; yet, at the same time, it made him anxious. He convinced himself that the next trade would have to be a loser. Allen was falling pretty to the gambling fallacy trap. This trap taunts an investor with the belief that after a string of winning trades (or losing trades) you will experience a string of losing trades (or winning trades). The result of falling into the gambling fallacy trap is creating a self-fulfilling prophecy. For Allen, this meant that his fear of losing became his reality.

In the United States, as soon as the market makes a significant upward move, the "prophets of doom" create a wave of market-crash and correction warnings, and before you know it, the major financial media is involved. Remember, on the eve of the 1987 crash, CNBC and financial media aired a special program to broadcast the "expected crash" right from the New York Stock Exchange? And of course, to fuel the anticipation, they began advertising the feature weeks in advance. Ten years later, on the anniversary of that day in October 1997, market analysts and fund managers were asked about the underlying reason for that historic market sell-off. Almost all of them said that they'd been surprised, that they had not found any significant factors contributing to the correction.

It is well worth noting here that there does not seem to be an inverse aspect of the gambling fallacy. In other words, while the standard trap is based on the psychological belief that "good things never last," there is no evidence of a prevalent inverse idea that, in a strong downward market correction, for example, the "bad things never last." This seemingly pervading cultural belief that "what goes up, must come down" creates the foundation for the gambling fallacy decision trap.

Consider applying the following methods to neutralize the impact of the gambling fallacy in your own trading:

- Realize that your trading system was *not* created based on the belief that "good things never last." Therefore, your system's recommendation is totally irrelevant to what you think or believe. Your thoughts and beliefs have already been accounted for in your system's performance, based on your unique criteria for either purchasing or developing it.

- If you notice that your interference with your system's recommendations is becoming more frequent after a series of wins, consider implementing a compensatory strategy to maximize your trading efficiency. A compensatory strategy is a tactic in which you delegate your trading responsibilities or decision-making to an objective outside party; for example, by having your broker trade your mechanical system for you.

b. The "hot-hand phenomenon" trap

To better understand the hot-hand phenomenon, take a quick glance at the theory of a "run" in statistics. Essentially, the theory asserts that in the course of a random act, you may see a series of favorable outcomes. Suppose you flip a coin 100 times. After a series of tosses, the coin turns up heads five times in a row. This repeated behavior, or "run," is sometimes referred to as a "hot hand."

Suppose you are in the market to purchase a mechanical trading system or subscribe to a trading advisory service. After only the most recent system or advisory results are presented to you, you conclude (or are persuaded), that the system is the holy grail you were always looking for or that the advisor knows what he is doing. But, unknown to you, the system just had a lucky run—a hot hand—which is not indicative of the genius of the advisor or the long-term profitability of the system. Yet this is a common scenario when mutual funds or other managed trading accounts are presented to clients.

Mark Hulber, publisher of the *Hulbert Financial Digest* offers a rigid statistical test known as the Runs Test. When applied to a set of data, the test helps objectively identify whether any simultaneous events represent a real run or a random run. He has applied what he's called the Runs Test to his 16-year database of investment newsletter performance and found

> "no evidence that any newsletter plays a hot or cold hand. Over the past 10 years we have performance data for 89 newsletters. Of those, three pass the test. But there's less here than meets the eye. At the 95 percent confidence level, you would expect 4 of those 89 to come out as false-positives. So far, for the 10-year period, there's no evidence of "runs of luck" or "runs of skill" either on the winning side or on the losing side. The data over the past 5 years presents the same picture: of the 219 portfolios for which the HFD (Hulbert Financial Digest) has data, 10 look like they had significant runs. But at the 95 percent confidence level you would still expect 11 of the 219 to come out as false-positives. So there's really no evidence that there are runs of luck or of skill among investment advisors." (8)

c. The "base rate" trap

Sometimes, an investor's reliance on representativeness causes him to ignore what's called the base rate: the probability of winning trades versus losing trades. Knowing system's base rate is critical, however, as it can make or break a trader's psychological ability to handle the system successfully.

Consider this example: The probability of an airplane crash is much less than a fatal car accident. However, several people are still fearful when boarding an airplane. By disregarding the base rate for an airplane crash, they raise the level of anxiety associated with air travel. Similarly, when a trader considers the purchase of a system and ignores the base rate, the psychological impact of that disregard is not realized until the trader is "under fire" and his or her performance suffers.

A trader I'll call Cliff, who once consulted with me, was very angry about a recent system purchase he'd made. He explained to me that his past five trades had been losers and said he no longer wanted to use the system. In discussing it further with him, I noticed that the base rate or probability of the system's winning trades were 20 percent. In other words, for each winner, he should expect to have four losing trades. I learned later that when he'd evaluated the system for purchase, he'd been attracted to the size of gain per each winning trade, but had ignored the base rate. As a result, he unnecessarily committed his funds to a system that was not compatible with his TPP (the psychological state that influenced his overall trading behavior); that is, psychologically, he just couldn't handle the 20 percent base rate.

This is why you should always consider the base rate before purchasing or designing a system. Personally, I don't favor any system with a base rate of less than 50 percent, since, in that case, flipping a coin could bring a higher success rate than following a system. However, lower base rates may be favorable and even appropriate for other traders and in other market situations. The bottom line is that you should consider the nature and tendencies of a selected market before committing to a particular trading system. That way, you won't commit your funds to a method incompatible with your trading psychology and become frustrated with your overall trading performance.

d. The "law of small numbers" trap

Another facet of the representativeness trap is the law of small numbers. The law of small numbers is the false belief that a small, random sample represents the population. As the psychologist Scott Plous explains, "The law of small numbers is a tongue-in-cheek reference to a law in statistics known as the law of large numbers." (3) The "law of large numbers" in statistics states that a sample size that adequately represents the whole has an average that is close to the population average. In other words, the larger the sample size, the closer its average to the population average. Tversky and Kahneman coined the phrase "law of small numbers" to refer to the tendency to draw conclusions based on a small, inadequate sample.

Once, I consulted with a trader named Allen, who was disappointed about his trading performance. When I asked him how he developed his system, he explained that a few times, he'd noticed that as soon as a particular technical indicator turned south, the market moved up a bit and then fell. As a result of that observation, he decided to use the indicator to generate trading signals for him. For a short time, his method worked, but as things progressed, he began getting several false or losing signals. Allen had fallen into the law of small numbers trap. He had become partially conditioned by giving too much weight to random outcomes, instead of back-testing his ideas with a larger sample.

In the next chapter, I will cover the subtle and sometimes not so subtle influences that frame dependence can have on both our trading performance and our everyday lives. But before I do, keep in mind that heuristic-driven biases and frame dependence do not play totally separate roles in affecting our decision-making; both enable an investor to identify the decision errors adversely affecting their investment performance.

Chapter 19 References

1. H. Shefrin, 2000, *Beyond Greed and Fear*, Harvard Business School Press.

2. Tversky and Kahneman, 1974, *Judgment under uncertainty: Heuristics and biases*, Science, 185, 1124-1130.

3. Scott Plous, 1993, *The Psychology of Judgment and Decision Making*, McGraw-Hill, Inc.

4. Leddo, Abelson, & Gross, 1984, Conjunctive explanations: When two reasons are better than one, *Journal of Personality and Social Psychology*, 47, 933–943.

5. J. Reason, 1990, *Human Error*, Cambridge University Press.

6. Ned Gandevani, 2002, *How to Become a Successful Trader—The Trading Personality Profile: Your Key to Maximizing Your Profit with Any System*, Writers Club Press.

7. Kahneman & Tversky, 1972, *Subjective Probability: A Judgment of Representativeness*. Cognitive Psychology, 3, 430–454.

8. "The Misuse of Past Performance Data," printed in *The Psychology of Investing*

Chapter 20:
Investment Decision Traps—
Frame Dependence

Frame dependence is making a decision based on how we see the given problem at that moment. Said in another terms, the way we perceive the issue at hand has a strong impact on what we decide about it.

Suppose you are in a long position and the market goes against you. Would you say they're pushing the price lower so the long position holders are stopped out, in other words taking the weak bulls out or that the market is starting a downward move? How you answer this question could determine how prone you are to the frame dependence trap. Let's say, in such a situation, your system sends you an exit signal, but you disregard it, rationalizing that they're taking the weak bulls out. Or, let's say your system continues to confirm your position, signaling for you to hold on, but you exit anyway, thinking the market is about to dip. You are falling into the frame dependence trap.

Framing traps have two basic variations: (1) frames as gains versus losses and (2) framing with different reference points.

1. Frames as gains vs. losses

The research of Daniel Kahneman and Amos Tversky has shown that, in general, we have risk-averse reactions to gains and risk-seeking reactions to losses. Put another way, in dealing with our gains and profits, we are quick to act to protect them (risk-averse). However, in dealing with our losses, we for some reason seem to want to hold onto them rather than getting rid of them, maybe in the pursuit of having control over a negative situation.

Studies of trading behavior dating back to 1940 portray this idea, projecting a rather gloomy image of individual investors who deal in different commodities markets such as S&P futures, oil, gold, and corn. Overall, when commissions were added to their totals for any given period, their losses for that period became substantially greater than their net gains.. More important, the studies concluded that an investor's average loss per trade was greater than the average gain per trade, and that traders often accepted substantial losses, even while their profits were small. In another similar study, Ray Ross discovered that, on average, losing trades were held twice as long as winning ones (1). And yet a third study confirms that investors tend to cut their profits short by selling their winners after making just a small profit while holding on to their losers (2).

One such investor, who we'll call Richard, placed an order to buy with great results: the market moved up, immediately giving him 2 points' profit. Anxious to stop while he was ahead, he quickly exited his position. Much to his dismay, anger, and sadness, the market kept going higher. "It was sickening to see that I could have made at least 12 points instead of a lousy 2," he said.

Shortly thereafter, the market gave him another signal to go long. He placed a long trade, accordingly, only to see the market drop 4 points below his entry level as he held his position. As the downtrend continued, he thought, *I need to manage my losses.* He had three choices as to how to do so: (1) to exit with a loss, (2) to do nothing and suffer, not knowing what fluctuations the market might bring, or (3) to buy more and then average in his price, hoping that the market would moved slightly back up. He took the third choice, and bought more, but the market continued dropping. Finally, when he couldn't take it any more, he exited with a substantial loss. He was furious knowing he could have exited much earlier and considerably reduced his losses.

Richard had fallen into the gains vs. losses trap: he was risk-averse with his profits and risk-seeking with his losses. Unfortunately, this trap is all too common; as an old saying goes, we hope when we should fear, and we fear when we should hope. To avoid the negative financial and psychological impact of falling into the gains vs. losses trap, consider the following:

- **Learn to deal with losses.** It is impossible to gain experience at winning trades without losing any. It would be like expecting to succeed at any endeavor without the associated obstacles and failures. (And if you hold such an expectation, you should seriously examine your beliefs, questioning where they came from, whether they're valid, and what results they've brought you.) As mentioned earlier, even when you think you have found the holy grail of investment systems, remember that history can always provide many examples to the contrary and that you could just be on a "run." One way to deal with losing trades is to expect every trade to be a loser. By accepting loss in this way, being always ready to deal with its consequences, you become pleasantly surprised by each winning trade.

- **Consider trading a business.** Regardless of how good a product or service might be, would you ever spend *all* of your money on it? Likewise, as a professional investor, you must consider each trade only one part of your business—not all of it.

- **Based on your trading behavior and TPP, evaluate whether the use of "mental stops" is appropriate for you.** For example, if you are slow to making decisions under stressful circumstances, mental stops might be your undoing. Certainly, you could say that by acting slowly, you have allowed enough wiggle room for your trade to gain profit; however, that wiggle room can also welcome enough loss to negate any benefits.

  More important, by obtaining good results from random behavior, you may become partially conditioned to believe you are on a "run" (see the hot-hand phenomenon described in the previous chapter) and that belief could spell disaster. Such partial conditioning can be seen in an individual who has won at a lottery or a slot machine a few times and so continues to buy lottery tickets or plug coins into the quarter slots, in the hopes of another win.

  In short, self-discipline is a critical requirement for a trader who wishes to use a mental stop in his or her trading strategies. So understand your personality and trading behavior when choosing such a vital parameter for your system.

2. Framing with different reference points

Here is a prime example of framing with different reference points: Richard's position in the S&P was under 4 points. Rather than considering this loss by itself, he compared it with his total equity. He would say, "this is only 2 percent of my total equity, so it should be okay." Let's review the variations of framing with different reference points.

a. The "anchoring" trap

Would you take a new sell signal when your previous short trade was a losing one? If your answer is no, you probably experienced the anchoring trap.

To demonstrate this concept, Hammond, Keeny, and Raiffa, authors of the article "Smart Choices," published in the *Harvard Business Review*, posed the following seemingly irrelevant questions to many groups over several years:

- Is the population of Turkey greater than 35 million?
- What's your best estimate of Turkey's population?

In only half of the cases, however, did the authors use the figure "35 million" in the first question; in the other half, they used the figure "100 million." The results?

"Without fail," the article states, "the answers to the second question increased by many millions when the larger figure was used in the first question."

In other words, if you're like most, the arbitrarily given figure in the first question would influence your answer to the second one.

In making decisions, we typically rely on the most recent information and data available to us, as it has the appearance of being more representative of the situation. As such, your initial feelings or thoughts, a recent news broadcast or magazine article, or a signal by your favorite indicator can all take the form of anchors.

The anchoring trap is one of the main reasons most forecasts by so-called experts turn out wrong. As the market goes up, these analysts expect a continued uptrend, and as it falls, a continued downtrend. In formulating predictions, they rely heavily upon current conditions and trends, such as those concerning a certain market or stock, while leaving future circumstances and elements little to no part of their analyses. The mutual funds industry, in particular, disguises this trap under the heading "past performance," advertising such biased analyses to promote their products

For stock investors, the anchoring trap often shows up in their like or dislike of a particular stock. Past winning trades can make them feel overconfident and careless, keeping them from participating in necessary due diligence before making their next trades. Conversely, when they have a few consecutive poor trades, they lose confidence in their system or analysis and begin seeking out a new holy grail. Some such investors virtually fall in love with their stocks, primarily for their past performance. Meanwhile, they neglect the company's current conditions and position in the overall economy and sector. And for day traders, who have to make numerous decisions throughout the day, the impact of anchoring is only magnified.

As an example, let's look at an investor named John. John recently had a great short trade, which has made him partial to short trades. He now neglects long trades and stays with the short ones longer than his trading plan dictates he should. He often wonders why he stays with certain trades despite new information from the market or from his indicators, but we can see it's because he's fallen into the anchoring trap.

In short, many types of investors, even those who could easily foresee other crucial elements in making trading decisions, fall into the trap of being anchored down to past trades. As a current or potential investor, you need to be aware of these anchors and attempt to minimize their influence in your trading decisions. Here are just a few ways to avoid them:

- Use a sound trading methodology or system that will limit spur-of-the-moment decisions based on emotions or hunches.

- Stand back and objectively question the validity of each of your decisions, analyzing each trade according to your method and asking yourself whether you'd go long or short at a certain juncture again. Then use your observations to gauge whether your next trade move is consistent with your methodology.

- Avoid any outside opinions and stick with your method. Remember, you've already worked hard to analyze your trading method and gained confidence in its signals. Asking others for their opinions or watching or listening to financial media are signs that you're looking for outside confirmation.

b. The "inertia" or "status-quo" trap

Rational decision-making is based primarily on two models: the Utility Model and the Probability Model. In the Utility Model we make decisions based on the utility or functionality of an alternative or based on the amount of desire we might have for that alternative. In the Probability Model, we weigh the outcome based on the assumed or known probability of the outcome. Using both models, then, we can determine and compare all of the possible outcomes or alternatives through various prices and formulas, and then choose the best possible scenario.

But both models have an inherent flaw: they assume humans to be rational beings. The reality, however, is that humans are emotional. Many studies, such as one by Dr. Joseph LeDoux (3), make it clear that our cognitive brain is inseparable from our emotions. Rational models for decision-making fail to incorporate that emotional factor.

Among our many emotional biases is the inertia or status-quo bias, which describes our general preference to stay with our previous decisions and positions rather than making new ones.

As a side note, one's susceptibility to the inertia trap should be considered when choosing between day trading and position trading. A day trader needs to make several decisions quickly, while a position trader often has a full day to make a decision. If likened to a video game, position trading would be Level I and day trading would be Level 9. Or, think of it this way: In a 1-minute chart of a security, there are around 405 bars. Now consider a daily chart of the same security, which has about 250 bars. These numbers indicate that trading a 1-minute chart as a day trader would for 6 hours and 45 minutes a day, 5 days a week, is essentially the equivalent of trading almost 2 years' worth of data. Therefore, after a battery of psychological tests, anyone with a high probability of falling into the inertia trap must avoid the pursuit of day trading.

Inertia bias is often reflected in an investor's "love my stock" attitude. That is, some investors seem to have strong emotional attachments to their stocks. They may rationalize their holding a favored stock longer than their system indicates by saying the stock is doing very well or was inherited from their grandparents, for example, regardless of its performance.

Let's look at Joe, for instance. Joe entered a short trade, and after initial fluctuation around his entry price, the market moved up a little. At that point, Joe considered exiting his losing trade when it hit his mental stop. But soon after, the market hastened up past his mental stop, and Joe just maintained his position.

"I could see the market was moving against my position," he said, "and I knew that when market passed my mental stop, I was in a bad trade. But I stayed with my losing trade anyway."

Joe was reluctant to exit because he was caught in the inertia trap. Just like all of the other traps, the inertia trap can be a symptom of larger underlying psychological issues that need to be dealt with. Was Joe procrastinating due to a fear of failure, for example? Was he displaying an avoidance behavior, trying to keep himself from making decisions so that he wouldn't later have to take any blame for being wrong? Was his reaction a sign that Joe doesn't like to be wrong and always strives for perfection? To ascertain the underlying problems, Joe's TPP should be analyzed. His TPP will identify possible decision-making pitfalls Joe may encounter and steer him toward a possible course of action to correct any underlying heuristics.

Now, consider Helen. Helen practiced her method on a simulative account known as paper-trading and began looking at the S&P market for almost a month.

Every day her chosen methodology worked well, and she came out a winner. Convinced that her method worked, she became confident and determined, and decided she finally felt comfortable enough to start trading her methodology with real money. One month later, however, she had not taken a single trade. She was, in truth, uncomfortable with her decision to go real-time or just too comfortable with paper trading. She was a captive of the inertia trap.

Also keep in mind that the inertia or status-quo trap is more pronounced when there is more than one choice to make. For example, if you wonder whether you should go long at a certain point or just wait for a better confirmation, once a better confirmation comes in, you're likely still waiting for another confirmation. To avoid this trap, one can do the following:

- Whether you have a mechanical system or a subjective methodology, understand and gain confidence in your trading method. This reduces the pressure on you to make constant decisions in order to validate your signals. The simpler your trading method, the easier it will be to stay disciplined in following the method, and the better your performance will be.

- Question your comfort zone. Maybe you need to adjust and expand your comfort zone regarding the type of market you're dealing with. If you'd like to avoid making decisions, for example, then maybe you should not be a day trader (4).

c. The "sunk-cost" trap

If the inertia trap continues for a while, it can lead into a second trap called sunk-cost. We have a strong tendency to make new decisions that justify and confirm and validate our previous decisions. This behavior becomes a problem when the previous choices are no longer valid.

This is a typical trap for investors and traders. Let's say we're long in a market, and as the market unfolds, we can see that our trade is no longer valid. But we refuse to exit and take a loss. Or if we had identified a profit target and, for some reason, the market is not quite reaching that level, we don't exit when we should. As a result, the market goes against us and our profit changes to loss, but we are reluctant to take a loss and prove that our previous decision is no longer valid. In fact, we may even continue to add contracts as the market falls, possibly hoping that by averaging our losses, we will somehow come out ahead.

Why is it that most of us cannot free ourselves from our past decisions? The answer to that question really depends on the meaning our past decisions hold for us as well as the impact they have in shaping our image of others and ourselves. Sometimes, breaking apart from our decisions seems almost impossible. But, as we have discovered, we can unlearn our undesirable behavior through a reflective learning process. To escape from the sunk-cost trap, in particular, we (and you) can do the following:

- Examine the underlying motives of your decisions. Is the purpose of your trading to prove you're right or to make money?

- Learn to admit your errors. Accordingly, consider whether your self-esteem is an area you may need to work on.

- Think in terms of probability. The outcome of any single trade or series of trades has no bearing in terms of long-term profitability (refer to the section about the gambling fallacy trap in the previous chapter).

- If necessary, reevaluate your trading system or methodology to ensure its compatible with your personality and risk tolerance (see the section about base rates in the previous chapter).

d. The "confirming evidence" trap

This bias leads us to seek out information that supports our existing point of view and, likewise, to avoid information that contradicts it. As such, the confirming evidence trap not only affects where we go to get information, but also how we interpret the information we receive. It also leads us to lend too much weight to supporting information, and too little to conflicting data.

A vast body of psychological research has supported the influence of emotions in making decisions. One particular behavioral model based on pain and pleasure clearly indicates our willingness to engage in activities that we like and avoid those that we dislike; as mentioned, this is the confirming evidence trap. Here are some examples of how this trap works in real-life scenarios:

- You're long for your trade, and you seek information to support this position. When the NASDAQ is rising, you feel good and want to stay long, although your methodology has nothing to do with the NASDAQ. You are seeking out any information that can validate your decision. Some time later, however, you notice that the NASDAQ is going south. This time, you say that you never thought the NASDAQ was important or exhibited a solid relationship with your market. Again, you are providing evidence that supports your wish to stay long. This is how we can be trapped by confirming evidence bias when we make decisions.

- You're long and you read something about current market conditions indicating that we're in a strong bull market where market is moving upward, and you believe it. Then you see that your original equity dropped 20 percent, but you justify that drop by saying "they're taking weak bulls, less capitalized investors and long position holders out."

- You're convinced of the seasonality index for a physical commodity like corn. Seasonality index projects possible future market moves based on previous calendar patterns. You trade based on that seasonality and go long on corn. A few days later, the crop report indicates we've produced too much corn and that China just dropped her contract to buy corn from the United States. You rationalize that the seasonality has worked for the past 50 years or so, which means the current situation only gives you a better chance to buy more corn at the lower price.

- Day traders who keep losing money after trying different trading methods question whether anyone can money in day trading; in other words, they question the validity of the practice. I've noticed this in some newsgroup discussions on Internet. A participant claims he is making money at day trading, and another person questions his honesty and integrity, immediately asking for proof such as account statements. This is a subtle form of the confirming evidence trap in which the second participant was seeking confirmation of his rationale about day trading and filtering out data that confirmed otherwise.

To avoid this trap, do the following:

- In the midst of real-time trading, do not factor in new elements or conditions that were not verified in your previous evaluation. Stick with your trading system.
- When you are in a trade, ask yourself whether you'd take the opposing position if you were not in your trade. If the answer is yes, you should re-examine your reasons for staying in your position.

e. The "mental accounting" trap

Traditional economic theory assumes that money is fungible (that one dollar can be used in place of another dollar). However, when individual behavior is studied, it appears money is slightly less than fungible.

Tversky would suggest putting yourself in the following scenario to determine whether you are prone to the mental accounting trap: Imagine going to see a play that costs $20 per ticket. When you arrive at the theater to buy the ticket, you discover that you have lost a $20 bill. Would you pay $20 for a ticket to the play? Eighty-eight percent of the respondents in his study would still purchase the ticket. However, the response changed when the problem was presented in this slightly different manner: Imagine you paid $20 for a ticket to the play. When you get to the theater, you discover that you lost the ticket and that the ticket cannot be reissued. Would you purchase another ticket for $20? Only 40 percent of respondents were willing to purchase another ticket.

There is no real difference between the two scenarios. However, in an irrational way, the outcomes appear to be different. For those who lost the ticket, the theater account was down $20. Purchasing another ticket would out the theater account down by $40, which was unacceptable to the majority of participants. But, for those who lost the $20, there was no effect on the theater account, so the cost of the play was still only $20. Rebalancing a portfolio is a practical application of this behavioral theory in finance. Rebalancing the portfolio to its target asset allocation often involves taking monies and allocating it to another asset class or investment manager that has not performed quite as well.

For a better understanding of how mental accounting could create a decision pitfall, consider the following example. You had great trading performance last week and are up about $2,000. But you just recently took a long trade and it is not working to your favor. You see that the market has passed your stop, but you refuse to exit your losing trade. You reason that you made $2,000 last week, so you have some room to let your trade ride. Your logic is that you're just playing with "house money." What you are really doing, however, is creating "mental" sub-accounts and then assigning different values to your sub accounts and the "house account." Therefore you are not considering the loss as yours, but as a loss against the house money. Meanwhile, you are ignoring all of the losses from your previous weeks of trading. To avoid such a trap, you can do the following:

- Evaluate each trade based on its own merits.

- Follow your system's recommendation for stops, regardless of how much you are up or down in your overall account.

While there are a few other traps you may have heard about that could influence our trading decisions, such as the "overconfidence" trap or the "prudence" trap, these traps are best identified through the TPP.

In the final analysis, however, remember that the simpler you keep your decision-making, the better your performance. In short, the more you analyze, the more you paralyze. In other words, create a system that works for you, and then do your best to take your system's recommended signals rather than acting out of emotional bias. By doing so, you will be well on your way to becoming a successful new-paradigm investor.

Chapter 20 References

1. Ross, 1975, Illinois Agricultural Economics, 27–31.

2. Braber & Odean, 2000, *The Journal of Finance*, 55, 773–806.

3. LeDoux, 1998, *The Emotional Brain*.

4. See the author's article "Do You Have Professional Potential? Eight simple points help you learn if day trading is for you," February 2003 issue of *Stock Futures &Options;* http://www.WinningEdgeSystem. com.

About the Author

Dr. Ned Gandevani is a professional trader and developer of the renowned Winning-Edge Systems, which is based on Chaos Theory. He holds an MBA and PhD in finance, and has coached professional traders for more than a decade. He has authored the trading-psychology book *How to Become a Successful Trader—The Trading Personality Profile: Your Key to Maximize Your Profit with Any System.* and *Trading Systems as A Determining Factor in Trading Performance* He has also written numerous articles for publications such as *Technical Analysis of Stocks and Commodities* magazine, *Futures* magazine, and *Stocks, Futures, and Options (SFO)*. He teaches graduate-level and MBA courses at Keller Graduate School of Management in Long Island and Manhattan.

Appendix A:
Investment Resources

Here is a list of Web sites and resources that can help you construct and managing your investment portfolio.

MSN Money (http://moneycentral.msn.com/investor/home.asp)
This site, part of the Microsoft Network, offers articles and advice on a wide variety of financial topics.

CNBC (http://www.cnbc.com/id/15839069)
Here you will find investing tools, stock screeners, a financial glossary, and fund information. It is provided by the CNBC cable channel.

Smart Money Magazine (http://www.smartmoney.com/smartmoney-magazine/)
This is the online version of the popular financial magazine. It is filled with helpful articles and practical tactics for investors.

Fidelity (https://www.fidelity.com/)
This Web site provides information about Fidelity's many products and services. Moreover, it contains tips for investment professionals and ordinary investors alike.

Vanguard (https://personal.vanguard.com/us/home)
This is the online home for the popular Vanguard family of mutual funds and ETFs. Not only can you manage your own accounts here; you can also learn everything you need to know about Vanguard.

iShares (http://us.ishares.com/home.htm)
The iShares Web site is specifically tailored for U.S. ETF investors. The site offers in-depth analysis and discussion.

State Street SPDRs (http://statestreetspdrs.com)
Offered by State Street Global Advisors. It features a plethora of funds and ETFs that any visitor can explore.

Morningstar (http://www.morningstar.com/Cover/ETF.html)
This popular site focuses on ETFs and provides a vast array of research and insights.

InvescoPowerShares (www.invescopowershares.com/)
Invesco PowerShares Web site currently features over 120 compelling investment opportunities through style, industry, commodities, currencies, specialty access, and broad market (ETFs).

Etfscreen (http://www.etfscreen.com/)
This is another ETF Web site. Among other things, it contains a performance comparison and an ETF screener.

TradeStation Securities (http://www.tradestation.com)
You can find good training tools here (such as a TradeStation simulator), along with some helpful information.

Yahoo Finance (http://finance.yahoo.com/)
This is a financial news Web site that carries pertinent stories for investors and people interested in personal financial issues.

Appendix B:
About Winning-Edge Investment Strategies
(www.winningedgesystem.com)

Winning-Edge Strategies offers a wide variety of trading courses as well as day, swing, and position trading signals. It also offers an appreciation of one of the most important trading components—your unique trading style and personality. In short, this site provides you with all of the crucial educational elements to make you a successful trader, including links to various articles and books. Browse through and take advantage of all of the outstanding features that Winning-Edge offers.

Trading Signals subscription services:

Day Trading Signals:

Subscribe to Winning-Edge Day Trading Signals to access our Web site each morning right after the market opens. Each signal is accompanied by a protective stop (of 2 points) and an initial profit target of 4 to 6 points.

Key benefits
- Web site is easily accessible with your password at any time and place.
- High percentage of winning trades (77percent in the last 64 months).
- Never a losing month in the past 5 years of the service.
- Small 2-point stop and average profits for 5 to 7 points per trade.
- Exact entry signals with stops and an initial profit target.
- Daily recap and reporting of the day's trades in the next day's posting.
- Each morning, one buy and one sell signal with a clear entry, a stop, and an initial profit target.

Swing Trading Signals:

Subscribe to Winning-Edge Swing Trading Signals to access short-term trading signals on the password-protected Web site every morning. Each day, after market triggered the signal , precise updates are posted on the Web to help you capture the maximum trading profits in a timely manner.

Key benefits

- Signals given via the Web site.
- Updates posted in a timely manner on the Web site for a high percentage of winning trades (70 to 80 percent).
- Exact entry, exit, stop, and trailing stop points.
- Daily recap and reporting of the day's trades in the next day's report.

Position Trading Signals:

While Swing Trading Signals are applied over a few days, Position Trading Signals, meant to appease the long-term investor, can hold their place in the market for 1, 2, even 3 weeks—or more.

Position Trading Signal subscribers receive a password to access our designated Web pages, which provide weekly updates on assumed positions and offer new buy and sell recommendations for major market indexes such as the S&P 500. Position Signals give a macroeconomic outlook along with implications for the S&P market. These signals also include initial profit targets and suggestions for protective stops. Subscribers may use our signals to take positions in SPY (the symbol for SPDR) and QQQQ.

Key benefits

- Advisory pages for position signals can be accessed 24 hours a day via a password-protected Web site.
- Weekly updates help you take the most advantage of market conditions.
- A macro outlook of the economy is given, which is based on the Winning-Edge Strategy, a nonlinear chaos-based analysis.
- Major S&P Index Futures market covered.
- Simple and practical entry and exit signals.

Trading systems for purchase:

Winning-Edge Day System:

The Winning-Edge Day System, designed for the S&P Futures Market Trading System, is quite simple, avoiding complex calculations and procedures. My proprietary technical indicator aids in locating objective key points that could offer profitable trading opportunities. The indicator, programmed for Omega Research TradeStation, may be programmed for other popular charting platforms as well.

There are typically 2 to 4 signals generated by Level 1 strategy each day. Each trade gives a target profit of about 4 to 10 points ($1,000 to $2,500). The protective stops are technically based and typically vary from $250 to $750 per trade for one big S&P contract. The system is based upon a combination of trend-following techniques and momentum expansion.

Key benefits

- Comprehensive manual.
- Precise, objective entry signals.
- Clear exit signals.
- Average risk and stops of 2 to 3 points.
- Average profits of 5 to 7 points.
- Typically trades for 2 to 5 times a day.
- Training course available in person, over the phone, or on the Internet.
- Training is one-on-one, providing a relaxed environment and the full attention that each student needs.

Winning-Edge Swing System:

The Winning-Edge Swing Trading System is designed to take the most advantage of short-term market swings. If you are a part-time or a full-time trader, you can enjoy trading futures and stocks with great profit. The system can be used to trade the S&P, Dow, and NASDAQ futures, as well as popular stocks such as Spiders (SPY), Diamonds, and QQQQ.

You don't need to be constantly glued to your computer. Just spend a few minutes every day to get all you need to trade your favorite stocks for a profit.

The Winning-Edge Swing Trading System is quite simple, avoiding complex calculations and procedures. My proprietary technical indicator aids in locating objective turning points—Swing Key Points—that could offer profitable trading opportunities. The indicator, programmed for Omega

Research TradeStation, may be programmed for other popular charting platforms as well.

Key benefits

- Comprehensive manual.
- Precise, objective entry signals.
- Clear exit signals.
- Average risk and stops of 3to 5 points.
- High number of winning trades.
- Typically trades 2 to 5 times a month.
- Training course available in person, over the phone, or on the Internet.
- Training is one-on-one, providing a relaxed environment and the full attention that each student needs.

Winning-Edge Position System:

The Winning-Edge Position Trading System is designed to take the most advantage of long-term market moves. If you are a part-time or a full-time trader, you could enjoy trading any futures or stocks with great profits. The system can be used to trade S&P, Dow, and NASDAQ futures as well as popular stocks such as Spiders (SPY), Diamonds, QQQQ, and currency markets.

You don't need to be glued to your computer. Just spend a few minutes every once in a while to get all that you need to trade your favorite stocks for profit.

The Winning-Edge Position Trading System is quite simple, avoiding complex calculations and procedures. My technical indicator aids in locating objective turning points—Position Key Points—that could offer profitable trading opportunities. The indicator, programmed for Omega Research TradeStation, may be programmed for other popular charting platforms as well.

Key benefits

- Comprehensive manual.
- Precise, objective entry signals.
- Clear exit signals.
- High number of winning trades.
- Training course available in person, over the phone, or on the Internet.

- Training is one on one, providing a relaxed environment and the full attention that each student needs.

Winning-Edge Forex System:

Forex trading offers many great benefits that can help you to achieve financial independence. With about a $2 trillion size, this trading market is the biggest worldwide.

Key benefits

- Low risk and high profit—The system's highly accurate signals help you achieve your financial goals with low risk and high profit.

- Precise entry and exit prices—No winning system could be easier and more precise than the Winning-Edge Forex. The proprietary indicators for TradeStation paint price bars and entry prices that you should buy or sell your favorite Forex market.

- Full-time or part-time trading—With the Winning-Edge Forex System, you could trade part-time or full-time via the Internet, 24 hours a day from anywhere.

- Day trade, swing trade, or position trade—The amazingly robust characteristics of the Winning-Edge Forex System allow you to choose your favorite Forex market for any time frame that you feel most comfortable with.

- High leverage—Many Forex brokers offer up to 100:1 and 200:1 leverage.

- Liquidity—With a daily trading volume of about $2 trillion, one cannot find a more liquid market.

- No commission trading—There is no commission charge for trading the Forex market. This is due to the fact that the broker pockets the difference between the bid and the ask price.

Subject Index

B

C

L

Large numbers, law of, 178
Law of small numbers, 178
Lehman Brothers Holdings, 27–28
Levels
 confidence, 177
 resistance, 116, 122
Life
 career, 40
 financial, 40, 48
Life cycle, ix, 40–41
Lifestyle, 11–12, 42
Liquidity, 31, 64, 77, 82–83, 101,
 116, 201
Long position, 131, 150, 153, 160,
 162–63, 165, 167, 181
Long-term corporate bonds, 85, 94
Losing, 31, 57–58, 62, 68, 77, 84,
 99, 145, 176–77, 182–83
Losing trade, 149, 171, 174–75,
 177–78, 182, 186, 190
Losses trap, 182
Love my stock attitude, 186
Low risk tolerance, 68
Lower risk tolerance, 37
Lynch, Merrill, 27–28, 106

M

Mac, Freddie, 27–28
MACD (Moving Average
 Convergence and Divergence),
 xi, xiv, 124, 128-129
Mae, Fannie, 27–28
Margin, 101, 154, 161, 163
Market
 financial, 85, 145
 international, 64, 99, 102, 104
Market behavior, 63, 117–18
Market conditions, 29, 34–35, 90,
 139, 144, 155, 174, 189
 real-time, 139
Market correction, 21, 25, 30, 62,
 82
Market hours, 35, 99, 101
Market indexes, 35–36, 85, 100,
 102, 121, 198
Market interest rate, 80–81
Market order, 154–55
Market participants, 24, 115–16,
 131, 140
Market price, xiv–xv, 31, 130, 132,
 150, 154–55
Market risk, 61, 83
 stomach, 62
Market segment, 99, 102
Market set-up, 140–41, 144
Market Technician Association
 (MTA), 193
Market type, 84–85
Market value, total security, 163
MAs, xi, 121–22, 124, 147, 150
 200-day, 122, 147–48
Materials, basic, 102, 104
MBA, 42, 45, 47, 193
MBSs (mortgage-backed securities),
 77
Measure, risk components
 attributes, 74
Measure risk, 65
Mechanical system, 139, 141, 172,
 174, 176, 187
Methodology, 138, 185, 187–88
Methods
 effective, 104–5
 risk-management, 57
Midfifties, 40
Midsixties, 40
Midthirties, 39–40
Mindset, 48, 138
Moderate, 68–69, 73, 158

P/E, 108
Pension fund portfolio, 27
Personal bankruptcy filings, 17
Personal Disposable Income (PDI), 4
Personality, 66, 69, 72, 180, 183, 188, 197
Philadelphia Stock Exchange, 100
Planning
  financial, 43
  long-term, 29
Portfolio, xi–xii, xv, 22, 69, 76–77, 87–91, 93–95, 97, 99–100, 102, 104–5, 108–11, 115, 122, 156–60, 164–65
Portfolio diversification, 83, 87
Portfolio focus, 41
Portfolio performance, 144
Portfolio return, 36, 88, 97, 159, 165
  expected, 159
Portfolio risk, 91
Portfolio strategy, 69
Portfolio turnover, 110
Portfolio value, 22, 105
Portfolio volatility, 73, 158
Portfolio's holdings, 34
Portfolio's maximum performance, 34, 97
Portfolio's performance, 160, 174
Position signals, 198
Position trade, 201
Position trader, 186
Position Trading Signal, 197–98
Positions, xv, 19, 33, 116, 118, 121–22, 131, 136–37, 144–45, 147–48, 150, 153, 181–82, 186, 188–89, 198
  portfolio's, 144
  profitable, xii, 147, 149, 156
  short, 63, 123, 131, 136, 145, 147, 150, 154, 160–61, 163, 166

Precious metals, 36, 56, 58, 77, 86, 101, 104
Prepayment risk, 81
Price, xv, 6–7, 9, 11–12, 14, 30, 35, 58–59, 78, 82–84, 116–18, 129–30, 133–34, 147–50, 153–56, 181–82
  bid, 154
  high, xiv, 117
  initial, x, 67
  low, 117, 126
  purchase, 150, 166
  security's, 144, 153–54
Price action, 117–18, 125
Price bar, 142–43, 146
Price behavior, security's, 116
Price ceiling, xiv, 91, 116, 120
Price chart, 117, 130–31
  security's, 116
Price correction, 166–67
Price level, 118, 131, 136, 142, 149
Price movement, 129, 131
  security's, 148
Price point, xi, 121, 126, 139–41, 150, 155
Price-to-book value, 108
Price-to-book value, low, 108
Price-to-earning value, 108
Probability, 57, 133, 143, 172, 177–78, 185, 188
Probability model, 185
Problem, 7, 13, 16, 22, 29–30, 115, 173, 175, 181, 186–87, 190
Products, 3, 103, 183–84, 195
  agricultural, 104
Profile, 67, 173–74
Profit, 22, 29–31, 35, 63–64, 82, 115–17, 121–23, 131, 136, 141–42, 144–45, 149–50, 153–55, 166, 180–82, 199–200